HANDBOOK FOR CREATIVE TEAM LEADERS

In memory of J. Daniel Couger and Peter Eliot

HANDBOOK FOR CREATIVE TEAM LEADERS

Tudor Rickards
Susan Moger

Gower

Published by
Gower Publishing Limited
Gower House
Croft Road
Aldershot
Hampshire GU11 3HR
England

Gower
Old Post Road
Brookfield
Vermont 05036
USA

British Library Cataloguing in Publication Data
   Rickards, Tudor, 1941—
   A team approach to creativity
   1. Teams in the workplace 2. Creative ability in business
   I. Title II. Moger, Susan
   658.4'02

ISBN 0 566 08051 6

Library of Congress Cataloging-in-Publication Data
Rickards, Tudor.
      A team approach to creativity / Tudor Rickards, Susan Moger.
         p.   cm.
      Includes index.
      ISBN 0-566-08051-6 (hardback)
      1. Teams in the workplace. 2. Creative ability in business.
   I. Moger, Susan. II. Title.
   HD66. R45 1998
   658. 4'036—dc21
                                                              98-27583
                                                              CIP

Typeset in 10/13pt Plantin Light by Wearset, Boldon, Tyne and Wear and printed in Great Britain by MPG Books Ltd, Bodmin.

CONTENTS

LIST OF FIGURES

FOREWORD

by Fran Cotton, Managing Director, Cotton Traders Limited

As anyone will know who has played a competitive sport, individual talent alone is not enough. Creative teamwork is a vital ingredient for success. That was my experience throughout my career in Rugby Union, where I was privileged to play with and against some of the outstanding teams of our generation. I also met some outstanding leaders. Later I became involved in the administration of the sport, where I sometimes feel that creative leadership is at least as important, and at least as rare, and where it is perhaps more difficult to maintain a reputation as a successful leader and team motivator.

I can certainly confirm this as the founder of an innovative business, Cotton Traders. To establish a business over a ten-year period with a small team of people who are still the heart and soul of Cotton Traders has been particularly satisfying. The seven factors of creative teams described in this book can serve as a checklist of features that business directors ignore at their peril. It also becomes clear why business, like competitive sport, runs smoothly only with the cooperation of motivated colleagues.

In my own business I am especially aware of the importance of 'shared vision' and 'ability to learn from experience'. A striking illustration is our Strategic Planning Process, which initially involved only the directors. Now our senior managers participate and input is required from every member of staff. The commitment to achieving our plans has been transformed by a shared vision and an ability to reflect on previous experiences.

I have another reason for commending the system proposed in this book. As a businessman based in the North-West of England I, like many other executives, have gained from contacts with Manchester Business School (MBS), the region's premier business school. One of my most enjoyable and enlightening experiences was to act as sponsor for a group of graduates from the school who worked with my management team on new ideas for Cotton Traders. In a short space of time we had formed a cohesive team from Cotton Traders and MBS. The ideas that emerged were both challenging and easy to test, and in the following months we developed several of them to advantage. Reading this book will indicate the kind of team training that had already been undertaken to enable us to achieve that result. Like many other business accomplishments, creativity may look natural but is often the product of intelligent application of a well-drilled set of routines.

Corporate executives, administrators and perhaps even leaders on the sports field will all benefit from a study of the *Handbook for Creative Team Leaders*.

PREFACE

This book offers a new approach which can enable teams of all kinds to achieve their creative potential. After reading it you will be able to recognize the features that differentiate dream teams and decide what might be done to improve performance in your own teamwork. If you are a specialist team leader or facilitator you will be able to apply new strategies and techniques for empowering and motivating team members, and for encouraging team development. You will also learn how to bring a more creative dimension to other approaches for improving team skills that have already been introduced into your work environment.

The origins of our study

For some years our working lives have been occupied by two related kinds of project. We have studied the behaviour of teams to understand how they approached their work tasks. And we have worked as part of many more teams as consultants and trainers with responsibilities for stimulating their creative outputs in terms of new and improved products, processes and strategies. In one or other form we have been involved with over 2 000 different work teams from 40 different countries, and across most organizational classifications.

All the examples in this book have been authenticated in at least one of the following three ways. The first approach has been based on interviews with team members and leaders. The second source of information has been from consultants, practitioners and researchers who share our interest in creativity and innovation management. We have given preference to those with whom we have worked, and with whom we have corresponded regularly. The third approach has been through direct involvement with the teams as trainers or facilitators.

An unexpected and puzzling discovery

In the course of our work we hit on an unexpected discovery. We came to the conclusion that most teams could be reliably classified into one of three discrete categories that could be differentiated on all of seven factors which we describe in this book. We termed the categories dream teams, standard teams and teams from hell. Such clear-cut discrimination across such a range of factors rarely occurs in exploratory studies. What made it more puzzling was our failure to find any satisfactory explanation in theories of team dynamics. It began to look as if the prevailing theories were at the very least incomplete.

An extension to theories of team dynamics

We later identified a way of explaining our practical findings through extending the well-known stage model of group formation. In its customary form, the theory suggests that groups go through a sequence of form, storm, norm and perform. Our extension is to identify teams from hell as ones that never escape the storm stage; standard teams as those that perform according to established norms; and dream teams that go beyond the norms of standard group behaviours. We now see the achievement of outstanding performance as arising from a form of team behaviour that combines learning and creating processes, triggered by the purposive actions of a creative leader (see Figure P.1). These findings make up the theoretical novelty which we report in these pages. Its practical implications are new and powerful ways of identifying team performance and influencing it.

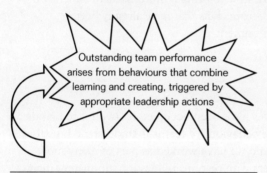

Outstanding team performance arises from behaviours that combine learning and creating, triggered by appropriate leadership actions

Figure P.1 Team performance: the basic premise

The stars of the show

The heroes and heroines of this book are members of teams that consistently produced results far exceeding what might have been expected of them. We refer to them as dream teams. These teams were found in small and large firms alike. We discovered small firms where a strong family culture is combined with a fierce determination to excel. We also came across excellent examples of creative team performance in global giants such as Procter & Gamble, Sony and Motorola.

The heartland of our work has been in UK-based organizations, including one of the largest police forces and one of the fastest growing web-based marketing operations. We have also collected information from creative leaders operating within the US and Norwegian military and in a public utility in the Netherlands. These teams give the lie to the notion that creative teams only exist in a narrow band of high-technology companies.

The contents of the book

Our study of creative teams complements work on the nature of creativity in the workplace described in the text *Creativity and Problem-Solving at Work*. In that book, the emphasis is on the application of a wide range of creative problem-solving techniques. Here we switch attention to the processes of team-building and productivity. Key techniques are described as means of stimulating team insights and of sustaining motivated team performance.

The book is in three parts. Part I deals with the basic principles that influence team performance. Part II describes our well-tested method for training teams to become more creative in their behaviours. Part III gives a range of examples of creative dream teams. All illustrate the principles that we believe differentiate dream teams from less successful ones. The final chapter includes examples of teams applying our recommended training approach.

The key findings reveal seven factors, all of which were more in evidence in dream teams than in all other teams. Some of the factors were already well known and expected. These include a strong, shared vision of what the team aspires to, a positive creative climate and persistent learning from experiences. Other factors are not so well known. Of these, the importance of building a platform of understanding has not been emphasized in earlier studies, nor has the impact of networking experts whom we call network activators.

In addition we report the role of creative leadership that offers prospects of increasing the performance of teams to dream team quality. This is important, as identifying team factors is only a valuable process to the extent that we can influence those factors positively. Creative leadership requires a commitment to 'win-win' or inclusive behaviours. The style is empowering and motivating so that team members acquire an enthusiasm for creating new ideas and for learning through experience.

A structured approach to creative team development

Creative leadership can be supported by systematic methods for stimulating creativity and learning. Our recommended approach, developed through many practical trials, is the MPIA system (Mapping, Perspectives, Ideas in Action). We outline its use both in order for the team to create valuable and useful ideas, and also to increase awareness and learning about team dynamics that help or hinder creative performance.

Who should read the book?

This book contains valuable information for anyone involved in work teams in their various shapes and forms. It also offers suggestions for management trainers, consultants and team facilitators. We have written it so that experienced team leaders may select elements and incorporate them into their prevailing approaches. Alternatively, the information on the MPIA system may be applied as a coherent system for structuring teamwork in order to achieve more creative results.

The range of examples indicates that creative teamwork is a necessity for success in a wide variety of organizational settings. We hope these accounts will encourage others to set themselves standards of teamwork that 'go beyond the standard', to achieve creative and exceptional results.

Tudor Rickards
Susan Moger

ACKNOWLEDGEMENTS

We are grateful for the support and help we received from many sources, without which this book would never have been completed. Although not mentioned by name, many of our colleagues, participants in teams described in these pages, and consultancy sponsors have given invaluable help. In addition, at Gower Publishing, Malcolm Stern and Solveig Gardner Servian were always helpful and demonstrated their high levels of competence and Genevieve Clarke's comments contributed greatly to the clarity of the text.

Fran Cotton, as well as providing us with a role model of a creative leader, kindly contributed the Foreword at a time of considerable work pressures.

Ian Newsome of West Yorkshire Police made constructive comments on the contents of an early draft, as well as on the material on the West Yorkshire facilitation project. Dr Jeremy Robinson also helped us clarify and bring focus to our ideas. Nick Gray has supported us for many years.

We wish to thank our interviewees, including Richard Hawksworth of Top Jobs on the Net; Dawn Gibbins and Mark Greaves of Flowcrete; Mary Wallgren of Procter & Gamble; Jeremy Kearns and Tony Price of Lancashire Dairies; Vivek Agarwalla, Muriel Causeret, Aditya Gandhi, Godfrey Kiiza and Vineet Mehea of the Lancashire Dairies Creativity Challenge team; Peter Casey and Rupert Jorissen of Casey Group; John-Christophe Barland of SmithKline Beecham; and Hugo Steven of ICI.

David Jardine and Debi Williams of Arthur Andersen, Tim Hamilton of Garretts and Jim Stockton of Manchester Airport have worked with us on the Creativity Challenge. We thank them and their organizations for their support.

Katherine O'Sullivan provided considerable moral support when deadlines loomed.

Our families have shown remarkable understanding of our preoccupations over the period when we were preparing and writing the book.

All these people, and many more, have enriched our thoughts and actions. We naturally accept responsibility for the sense that we made and then expressed in these pages.

TR
SM

PART *I*

CREATIVE TEAMS IN PRINCIPLE

1 AN ANATOMY OF TEAMS

An insight into team performance

A few years ago we hit on a powerful insight about teams. We concluded that almost all teams fitted into one of three, easy-to-identify, categories which were differentiated by seven factors. It also became clear that teams performed as if there were barriers that were hard to break through on all seven factors. We later came to the conclusion presented in this book, that team performance on all these factors could be improved through deliberate interventions by a team leader. The insight required us to modify our understanding of a well-known model of group formation.

The three team categories

The first category contained a small number of teams with great team spirit that demonstrated sustained outstanding performance. We began calling these the dream teams. The second group, and by far the largest, contained standard teams. The final group, fortunately with the fewest examples, was made up of what we came to call teams from hell.

As we began looking more systematically at team behaviours, evidence accumulated in favour of the three categories. For example, when we described them in our consultancy and training work, there was widespread support for our idea. We are now confident that the overwhelming majority of professionals and managers are able to recognize the three groupings from their personal experience of teams.

Our explanation for our findings begins with the well-established notion that group formation passes through the stages form, storm, norm and perform. We now believe that our teams from hell never proceed beyond the storm stage. We also believe that the theory needs an additional stage. Dream teams pass through the storm, form and norm stages, and then outperform standard teams by challenging the norms they have previously established.

AN EXAMPLE OF A DREAM TEAM

One Saturday evening, a chief executive officer stood helplessly by and watched her main manufacturing plant destroyed by fire. She was one of the first eyewitnesses on the scene. Within hours many of her employees had made their way to the site. There followed a weekend of round-the-clock efforts. By the following Monday morning staff were operating from a mobile office shell, reassuring anxious customers they would be able to complete their orders. The commitment of the team transmitted itself to the customers, and not a single order was lost. The company has since gone from strength to strength. This is but one example of the exceptional and sustained efforts we have come across in dream teams.

AN EXAMPLE OF STANDARD TEAMS

A global organization runs an annual competition to reward its most innovative teams. Each division has to submit a nomination, describing the achievements of the team during the year and providing an indication of the general team processes. Typically the judges have a hard time distinguishing between the performance of most of the entries and the general quality is high. After all, this is a successful international company. This has good and bad aspects to it. Only in unusual circumstances do its teams deviate from the standard or norm. The similarity in performance across divisions is an excellent illustration of how an organization expects, and thus gets, a certain standard of performance.

AN EXAMPLE OF A TEAM FROM HELL

In November 1990, Britain watched in growing amazement as Sir Geoffrey Howe addressed a packed House of Commons. In quiet and controlled tones he unleashed a devastating personal attack that was to lead to the rapid overthrow of Prime Minister Margaret Thatcher. The unusual aspect of the confrontation was that the speaker was a former member of Mrs Thatcher's own top team of cabinet ministers. Mrs Thatcher, for all her international reputation, had evidentially presided over a classic team from hell.

Are there glass ceilings to team performance?

When we start discussing these three classes of teams, we are asked one question before any others. Can teams change their standard of performance? Might there be versions of the famous 'glass ceiling', as shown

NOT ALL TEAMS ARE EQUAL

In our work with one global organization, we noticed a remarkable uniformity of performance demonstrated in teams across all the divisions of the company. The corporate culture seemed to establish expected norms of behaviour which were reflected in the team reports of their innovative achievements. Most teams stuck to those norms.

However, even within this organization, we would sometimes come across examples of non-standard teams. One year, for example, the clear winner of the innovation award was a team that had established a manufacturing plant in a remote region of China, overcoming a thousand unexpected difficulties. The judges were unanimous in recognizing this dream team.

In complete contrast, in that same year, another team submitted an entry that read like an organizational suicide note. 'We didn't complete our project due to unforeseeable circumstances,' the team reported. A catalogue of excuses was made for the team's poor performance, with hints at unfair treatment, lack of resources and internal wrangles. The judges were well aware of the team's circumstances and found the excuses unconvincing. Not only did the team perform poorly; it seemed quite unable to understand the reasons for that poor performance. As we will see, a lack of self-awareness of this kind is one of the features of a team from hell.

In this one organization we see how a corporate climate establishes norms of performance expected of its teams. The standard team behaviours are almost universal. However, there is still scope for exceptional performance and dream team behaviours will shine out in contrast.

in Figure 1.1, barring teams from hell from reaching modest standards of performance, and barring standard teams from becoming dream teams?

The short answer is yes – there are such barriers. The evidence we have collected shows that, time and again, dream teams go on being dream teams and standard teams persist in their standard level of performance. The longer answer is that the barriers are real, but to some degree imposed by the teams themselves. The glass ceilings can be shattered. One saying sums up the self-imposed nature of the glass ceiling to team performance, as a step to doing something positive about it. As shown in Figure 1.2, this is

If you always do what you've always done –
you'll always get what you've always got.

The search for team improvement turns out to be one in which 'always doing what we've always done' becomes clearer, so that the team can consider other ways of doing things, and other things to do.

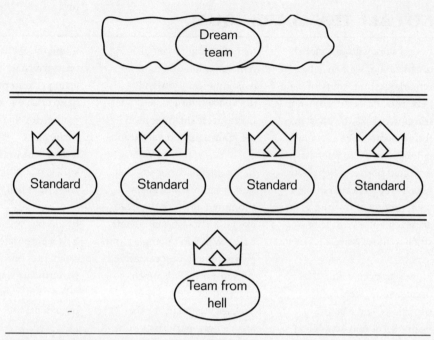

Figure 1.1 Team types and glass ceilings

Figure 1.2 Why teams do not change

To identify the glass ceiling, and what might be done to shatter it, we will first summarize those patterns of behaviour that distinguish the three types of team.

Seven factors that shape team performance

We believe that there are seven factors by which dream teams may be distinguished from teams from hell. Most of them can be found in one form or another in other studies of team behaviours and it is highly unlikely that one set of factors, ours or anyone else's, will serve for all kinds of team. Our only claim for the list we are about to provide is this: the factors were derived from our experiences of working with many organizations in efforts to improve the creative performance of their teams. As a consequence we have identified connections between the factors and practical steps for achieving team development.

Figure 1.3 shows the seven factors as they appear in the extreme kinds of team, dream teams and teams from hell. These somewhat exaggerated contrasts are a good way of introducing the seven factors.

The seven factors are strongly interactive. That is to say, the dream teams score highly on all seven factors; the teams from hell come out poorly on all seven. Standard teams fit somewhere between the two extremes. For the moment we will concentrate on the dream teams and teams from hell and these give very clear indications of the seven factors.

Seven secrets of dream teams	Seven sins of teams from hell
Strong platform of understanding	Poor platform of understanding
Shared vision	No shared vision
Creative climate	Poor climate for creativity
Ownership of ideas	No ownership of ideas
Resilience to setbacks	Fatalistic to setbacks (scapegoats)
Network activators	Few networking skills
Learn from experience	Don't learn from experience

Figure 1.3   The seven secrets of dream teams and seven sins of teams from hell

THE 'ALL OR NOTHING' NATURE OF THE SEVEN FACTORS OF EFFECTIVENESS

It is not always possible to examine a team's characteristics on all seven factors from outside the team and at a given point in time. This restricts our claims to the status of a theory. When we have been able to collect information on all seven factors, however, the result has been clear cut: the performance is 'all or nothing' on all seven. It seems unlikely that one or more of the factors may be 'pulling' the others along and we have concluded that the factors are mutually reinforcing. They are signals of the team's general sets of behaviours, or norms. As we show, the extra ingredient necessary to influence all seven factors in the same direction is the leadership process.

Think of a team as a rowing boat, and the factors as rowers. Most teams have the factors operating according to the required procedures and to a given standard of performance. The team that achieves dream performance has successfully stepped up the pace and all seven rowers (factors) are performing in beyond-standard fashion.

The majority of teams operate under standard conditions. And 'if you always row like you have always rowed, you will always race like you have always raced' – until something happens. If one rower loses an oar the norms are swiftly disrupted and overall performance slips. Eventually the boat reaches a lower norm of performance all round; in other words, a standard team has drifted in performance after a setback.

Teams from hell never get their rowing pattern right. Whichever factor you study the signals are not good.

In teamwork, the old metaphor is very apt. All members are in the same boat.

PLATFORM OF UNDERSTANDING

The first factor differentiating dream teams from teams from hell is the presence of a strong platform of understanding. This has been largely ignored in other books about teamwork, although perhaps implied by notions of team learning. It refers to the powerful cohesive effect produced when team members understand and respect each other's viewpoints. Building a platform of understanding is a means of strengthening performance in the other six factors.

This concerns those aspects of team dynamics that are needed to achieve shared values, beliefs and goals. One of the most important principles of creative teamwork is developing mutual respect among team members. This mutuality principle is lacking in teams from hell and underdeveloped in standard teams. Structures for enhancing team creativity include techniques for strengthening this platform of understanding. Of specific importance is the 'Both And' or 'Yes And' technique through which team members are able to achieve win-win outcomes when engaged in team work.

SHARED VISION

All teams have shared responsibility for achieving something, even though the 'something' varies from team to team. Few teams are able to convert this responsibility into a shared vision that motivates and sustains team progress. Although shared visions are much talked about in organizational texts, the difficulty lies in avoiding lip service to a shared vision and in seeking a practical set of steps to identify one if it is suspect or missing altogether.

One of the triumphs of techniques for stimulating creativity is accumulating evidence that a team can take control over its own processes of seeking and discovering a shared vision, for instance by introducing metaphors into team discussions that lead to powerful and motivating images for the team. We will show in Chapter 3 how such visualizing metaphors can help to transform performance from standard to dream team levels. We also suggest that efforts to discover a shared vision have to be accompanied by similar efforts to achieve improvements in the other factors needed for sustained dream team performance.

TEAM CLIMATE

The third factor relates to the psychological climate for creative change within teams. Although the team climate seems to reveal itself in a number of interconnected ways, we are here concerned with the climate for creativity. This is a factor which has been repeatedly found in research studies to be an indicator of successful and innovative change.

In Chapter 2 we look at one of the best-established measures of creative climate which offers an excellent and easy-to-apply indicator. However, we see this factor as less easy to influence directly than some of the others.

OWNERSHIP OF IDEAS

The fourth factor concerns ownership of ideas. In dream teams the ideas that receive the greatest attention are those perceived as open to strong sponsorship by team members. This kind of approach reduces the gap between ideas and actions. Each team member is at the same time part owner of the shared vision, and is also looking for ways he or she can take ownership for smaller bits of the action. Our case studies give very clear examples of the way in which ideas become owned in dream teams and of the roles played by team members and sponsors in this process.

There is a clear distinction in attitude between teams where there is a 'doing with' attitude and those where there is a 'doing to' attitude. The 'doing with' attitude of dream teams is closer to ideas about networking – itself another of the factors of successful teams. The 'doing to' attitude is more common, and more typically associated with standard teams. It sometimes results in 'selling' an idea (or, in slightly more sophisticated form, in achieving 'buy-in').

RESILIENCE TO SETBACKS

The fifth factor is resilience to setbacks. Even dream teams sometimes try something that fails or run into a nasty shock that could not have been foreseen. In any event, the reaction is a flexible one. One successful management director cited resilience as the key feature that set his current team apart from most others.

Resilience is more likely to produce successful results if the team has a positive climate and a strong platform of understanding. In contrast, the teams from hell are quick to find 'causes' for failure that are beyond their control. We have already mentioned a team that tended to blame scapegoats for their difficulties.

NETWORK ACTIVATORS

The sixth factor is evidence that some of the team members – we call them 'network activators' – are particularly good at working with key individuals both within and outside the team. As ideas of networking become better understood, it seems likely that network activators have a rich set of contacts often operating outside formal organizational systems, exchanging ideas and generally offering mutual support. One of our examples describes the way that corporate entrepreneurs ('intrapreneurs') reach out and support each other across corporate lines. We devote Chapter 8 to this important factor, including the newly identified phenomenon of a network of mavericks.

REFLECTIVE LEARNING

The seventh of our factors deals with the abstract topic of learning, and specifically with the manner in which team members learn from their experiences – a factor requiring special attention. Without learning from experience, there can be little hope of developing and improving on the other six factors.

Creative leadership: the extra ingredient for team effectiveness

There is an extra ingredient required if a team is to progress towards dream team effectiveness. This is leadership which, as indicated in Figure 1.4, works its way into the team behaviours on all seven of the key factors. For us, the differentiating leadership style is that of creative leadership. Other authors have given effective leadership various names such as transformational leadership, situational leadership and empowering leadership. In fact, these different labels conceal much common ground. Our own perspective is to focus on the need for creativity in teamwork, and hence our preference for the term creative leadership.

Figure 1.4   The central role of creative leadership

A practical way to define creative leadership is to characterize it by its appearance in action. So, as a first step, we can say that it reveals itself in those actions of leaders that contribute to the performance of dream teams in achieving excellence.

FOUR FEATURES OF CREATIVE LEADERSHIP

A more formal definition needs to capture the essential characteristics. There are four features that can explain many of our practical observations of creative leadership.

1 A value set found in creative leaders which we have called the 'mutuality principle'. This implies that creative leaders believe in, and are always striving for, win-win or Both And outcomes in teamwork.
2 An empowering and motivating leadership style.
3 The deployment of strategies and techniques that encourage team members to learn and solve problems.
4 An alignment of individual needs and team tasks or responsibilities or, as we say, 'Hips and lips should be heading us in the same direction.'

All four features of creative leadership will figure prominently in the rest of the book as they relate to the seven factors found in dream teams. In the next section of this chapter we look at how, through creative leadership, teams might attain dream team status. In other words, we return to the problem of glass ceilings to team performance. In the final section, we introduce the creative problem-solving systems that were the precursors to the approach which we will be developing in subsequent chapters.

Beyond the glass ceiling of standard performance

Most textbooks describe team development as proceeding through the four stages of form, storm, norm and perform as in Figure 1.5. The form stage is when there is a period of orientation, with not a little sounding out and exploration of 'What's going on'. The storm stage is triggered when team members jockey for position in order to achieve personal goals and inevitably encounter conflict. At the norm stage team cohesion occurs which leads to effective problem-solving or the perform stage.

The theory is based on well-documented studies, although it is no longer widely reported that the definitive work was conducted on teams of juveniles in summer camp. We have never found it easy to pin down the stages in the teams we work with because activities often swing wildly backwards and forwards. Even if some general sense of progress from stage to stage is recognized, the time spent at each seems indeterminate at the start of any team exercise. Nevertheless, we find the model valuable for the questions it raises.

The general development proposed is one in which teams start like teams from hell and proceed to become dream teams. However, the model does not fit the world we occupy in that it assumes that progress is only a matter of time. As indicated in Figure 1.6, it is unable to answer the teams-from-hell question 'What happens if the storming persists?' Nor can it answer the question 'What happens if performance is unsatisfactory?'

In short, the model is too simplistic. It is strengthened if we build in glass ceilings restricting the progress of those teams not achieving dream team performance. For teams from hell, storms persist. That is sad, but at least the proportion of such teams is small. Even more seriously, we believe there is a ceiling for standard teams which, it will be remembered, make up the majority. The ceiling is implied in the original model.

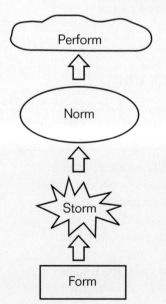

Figure 1.5 The FSNP team model

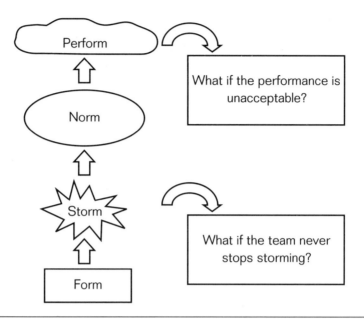

Figure 1.6 The unanswered questions of team development

For standard teams, action or performance is dictated by the norms established.

What is needed is a means by which the norms of group performance can be exceeded. We have already indicated that creative leadership is the way towards developing outstanding team performance.

Introduction to structured systems for developing a creative team approach

There are undoubtedly ancient accounts of systematic methods for seeking inspiration, for example, within Indo-Asian cultures. These might be taken as the first creative problem-solving systems.

In the Western world the strongest claim in modern times might be made for systems based on the apparently simple ideas of Alex Osborn, inventor of brainstorming, that are still attracting controversy half a century later. What is beyond doubt is that some form of idea management drawing on aspects of Osborn's original concept of team brainstorming can play a valuable part in the development of the skills necessary in a creative team.

OSBORN'S GIFT TO TEAMS FROM HELL

Osborn was all too aware of teams from hell. His observation of teams he worked with was vivid and convincing. He believed that they were often dominated by status, and were destructive of all but a few ideas that fitted in to the views of a handful of domineering individuals. Once again we have a description of teams permanently stuck in the storm stage of development.

Osborn's gift to these storm-bound teams was ironically another kind of storm, a set of rules for brainstorming. Above all, he urged a structure of deferral of judgement. We would say that this instruction might shift teams from hell temporarily up to the level of standard teams. Why temporary? Because the technique alone does not have the kinds of features required for creative leadership. Why only to a standard level? Because until the team members are operating to an even higher level of performance, there is little possibility of breaking out of norms or beliefs. Put another way, the rules of brainstorming may not be strong enough to change the norms of standard team behaviour. They certainly have little impact on teams from hell. We would argue that attempts to brainstorm creative ideas have to be accompanied by creative leadership

THE PARNES-OSBORN ARCHETYPE OF STRUCTURED CREATIVITY SYSTEMS

Osborn's legacy was an international institute for the study and promotion of creative behaviours. The Creative Education Foundation at Buffalo now attracts hundreds of people to its conferences, many of whom subsequently apply the ideas in their places of work and in their personal lives. Its basic system for creative teamwork is known as the Parnes-Osborn approach which was developed from Osborn's brainstorming, particularly by Sidney Parnes, who became President of the Foundation. Our suggested system for creative teamwork in this book owes much to this approach.

Of particular significance was the extension of creativity from an idea-finding stage to other stages of teamwork. This includes creating an understanding of the nature of the problem itself and of the dynamics of accepting ideas. In short, Parnes-Osborn teaches that for teams it is 'creativity all the way'.

THE ORIGINS OF VISUALIZATION IN TECHNIQUES FOR STIMULATING CREATIVITY

Sidney Parnes experimented with ways of making the Parnes-Osborn system more 'whole brain' and open to visualization. Other contributions showed that creative teams entered into a psychological state receptive to creative discovery. In studies with engineering design teams, the shift was marked by a change in vocabulary. The usual detached and analytical vocabulary ('left-brain') becomes richer in 'word pictures' that evoked visual thinking (more 'right-brain' contribution). These studies paved the way to techniques specifically designed to shift teams away from conventional thinking patterns towards temporary states of enhanced visualization. Examples of visualization in the intuitive behaviours of creative leaders will be found in the case studies. Suggestions for deliberate stimulation of visualizing metaphors by team facilitators are given in Chapter 3 and there are examples in action in Chapter 9.

CREATIVE ANALYSIS AS THE FOCUS FOR CREATIVE DEVELOPMENT

An important additional dimension to our work has been an attention to the processes of team development through an approach known as creative analysis, described in the companion book to this volume, *Creativity and Problem-Solving at Work*.

This might be seen as supporting the special kinds of learning needed for a team to develop its creative performance. Teams trained in creative analysis become more skilled at exploring the basis of their own creative efforts through experimentation with creativity enhancing techniques and then reflection of those processes in the light of experience. As a consequence, the norms of team behaviour are always open to revision and improving on standard performance replaces standard performance itself as a team norm. We might say that creative analysis establishes a 'norm to break norms' in its efforts to secure exceptional team performance. This brings us to the final refinement to the form-storm-norm-perform model as shown in Figure 1.7. The simple introduction of behavioural techniques might temporarily achieve standard performance in teams from hell. Systematic attention to team dynamics and to team performance will help standard teams shatter the glass ceiling and achieve dream team performance.

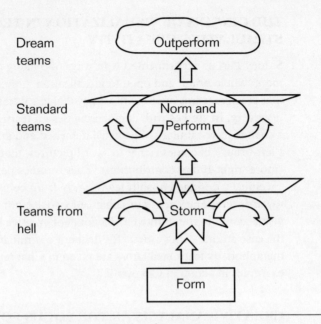

Figure 1.7   Going beyond standard performance

Summary

This chapter began by describing three types of team we had observed – dream teams, standard teams and teams from hell. The characteristic which marks the teams out from one another is the degree to which they show great team spirit and sustained outstanding performance. We pointed to the 'glass ceiling' effect, which can prevent teams from moving from one level of performance to another. However, the glass ceiling can be shattered by positive efforts to improve performance.

We suggested seven factors which help to distinguish dream teams from teams from hell: a strong platform of understanding, a shared vision of the ultimate goal, a creative climate, a willingness to take ownership of ideas, resilience to setbacks, the ability to activate networks and the capacity to learn from experience. The dream teams perform strongly on all these factors, the teams from hell poorly. Standard teams rate somewhere between the two extremes.

The extra ingredient for team effectiveness is creative leadership. Creative leaders are often recognized by their actions, and we describe four features which characterize them. These are a belief in mutuality (striving for win-

win outcomes); an empowering and motivating leadership style; the use of strategies to encourage team learning; and a constant check on the alignment between individual needs and team responsibilities.

The well-known model of team dynamics – forming, storming, norming and performing – describes stages in team development. To break the glass ceiling, however, we suggest a creative development approach in order to help members transcend the norms of group performance. The framework derived from the Parnes-Osborn approach is supplemented by attention to the process of team development known as creative analysis. This helps to establish 'norms to break norms' necessary for exceptional team performance.

2 BUILDING CREATIVE TEAMS: 'THE GENIUS OF THE AND'

American management researchers James Collins and Jerry Porras wanted to find out what differentiated visionary companies from the rest. These companies, which included Sony, 3M, Hewlett Packard and Procter & Gamble, were described in their best-selling book *Built to Last*. This remarkable and thorough study produced several unexpected findings. The companies did not necessarily have a charismatic leader, but a founder or successor with what we would call a creative leadership style that created open and dynamic learning systems capable of renewing themselves. One core value was dominant in the culture of such companies, described by the authors as 'the genius of the and'. We wish we had thought of that. Their term lies behind what we call the mutuality principle or, in other words, the possibilities of inclusion and win-win within teamwork.

This chapter concentrates on creative leadership and its consequences. We look at the core value of mutuality or 'the genius of the and', that is also the hallmark of creative and visionary leadership. We show how it promotes learning and creating, and we outline techniques for vision-building and idea development. We suggest ways in which the creative leader can directly encourage learning and creativity. These include support for more visual thinking; improved understanding of individual differences through team diagnostics; and a powerful yet simple technique for stimulating positivity and idea development (the Yes And technique).

Creative leadership and its consequences

In Chapter 1 we mentioned the four key features of creative leadership: a strong belief in win-win outcomes (mutuality); an empowering and motivating style; strategies that encourage creativity and learning; and a sensitivity to the balance between individual and team needs. Now we shall see in more detail how these features make a difference. Figure 2.1 shows a simplified picture of the consequences of creative leadership in the development of creative teams.

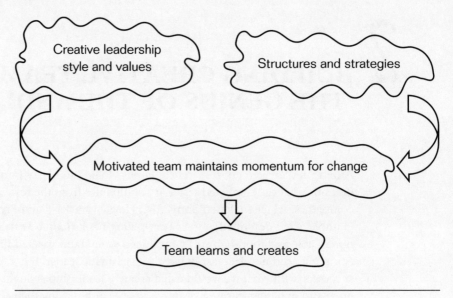

Figure 2.1   Creative leadership supports team learning and creating

Leaders set the team climate through their core values, among which mutuality is paramount. The leadership style is an enabling and visionary one through which team members have feelings of involvement rather than coercion. Strategies and structures are consistent with such a style so that the team has more opportunities for self-determined actions out of which grows motivation. To maintain that momentum the processes have to sustain creativity and learning.

The structures favoured by creative managers are those in which ideas flow freely, regardless of the status of individuals. The creative team leader acquires the role of coach or facilitator so that the structure permits involvement. The strategies are those that concentrate on the needs and goals of the team. We can summarize the consequences of creative leadership as the development of a motivated team engaged in its tasks so that creative outcomes and developmental learning are sustained.

CREATIVE LEADERSHIP, VISIONARY LEADERSHIP AND TRANSFORMATIONAL LEADERSHIP

Leadership remains one of the great unresolved puzzles of management. In countless articles and books we see three overlapping styles of leadership that are claimed to be powerful triggers of exceptional performance. As well

as creative leadership, there are visionary leadership and transformational leadership processes as shown in Figure 2.2.

Visionary leadership has been associated with an explanation of the special powers that a leader can exercise through a strong vision for change. The vision takes on a self-sustaining character – a special kind of shared mindset that inspires those touched by it. We also know that our dream teams are sustained by a shared vision.

Figure 2.2 Three overlapping leadership styles

The term transformational leadership tends to be set in opposition to traditional management methods, the basis of which is the agreement or transaction. A manager operates a form of control whereby those being managed do what is expected for an agreed reward. In contrast, transformational leadership encourages the breaking of old expectations or mindsets. In teamwork, this offers scope for the team to create some aspects of its future.

We can see how the concepts of visionary and transformational leadership point the way for teams to achieve substantial changes beyond the glass ceiling of standard performance. In this sense, the work on visionary and transformational leadership is important to our present concerns. Our own preference is to use the term creative leader, thus recognizing the visionary and transformational implications. It also avoids misrepresenting terms associated with other bodies of knowledge.

Mutuality: 'the genius of the and'

The multiple uncertainties of the information age are increasingly said to present mutually connected threats and opportunities. This is the ancient and revered value of mutuality of apparently conflicting forces. In Chinese philosophy this mutuality is believed to exist as a 'harmony of opposites', the yin-yang. However ancient, the principle of mutuality has never been more vital for our society, where people have lost the certainties of traditional jobs and working practices.

Edward de Bono, of lateral thinking fame, sees the principle as an epoch-making shift away from the rationality of 'either-or' logic towards new forms of logic that are fuzzier. In his book *I am right – You are wrong*, he writes of the new Renaissance as a move 'from rock logic to water logic'.

Some years ago a very gifted friend of ours, Dr Peter Eliot, was studying schizophrenics and had become fascinated by the apparent discontinuities in their logic. They seemed to make unexpected moves 'like knight moves in chess'. Together we developed an idea that under less extreme mental conditions, 'knight's move thinking' could help people break free from a pervasive weakness in everyday thinking that reduces complexities into a series of either-or steps. If I am right and you disagree, you are wrong. Either that or you are right and I am wrong. In knight's move thinking, attention is directed to finding out how both of us can escape the either-or, right-wrong trap.

Creative leaders are sensitized to such opportunities for win-win. Furthermore they watch out for ways in which a team can become bogged down with debates over either-or, and when knight's move thinking is called for, as in Figure 2.3. The watchword might well be 'There must be other

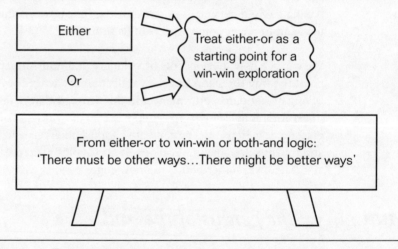

Figure 2.3　The mutuality principle and either-or logic

ways . . . There might be better ways' – in other words, an expression of belief that oppositions can usually be reconciled through creative effort. The slogan is one of the most valued 'takeaways' from our courses and is often displayed prominently where a team can refer to it in subsequent conferences and meetings.

MUTUALITY IN CREATING AND LEARNING

The most obvious way that mutuality supports creativity and learning is in the factor 'learning from experience'. Here the mutuality principle helps to focus on a special kind of learning in which doing, and thinking about what is being done, are mutually reinforcing. Some years ago the process was described as a learning cycle, pioneered by Professor David Kolb, in which a specific experience offers 'food for thought' or reflection. This can suggest a more general concept about the experience, which in turn suggests different ways of operating in future. The original learning cycle did not clarify learning about tasks and team behaviours, so we have built these in, as shown in Figure 2.4.

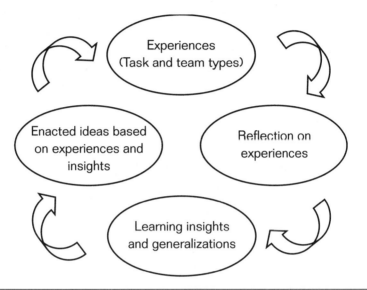

Figure 2.4   The reflective learning cycle

The team acquires the habit of reviewing its experiences on a regular basis. At each review session the members consider what has happened. For example, after a brainstorming session, the team will assess the quality and workability of the ideas produced. Is the team on track and progressing towards its goals? In addition it will also consider the processes and techniques used. Did all members contribute? Did any member dominate? Should it try some new approach? As a consequence of this reflective process, the team may decide to experiment with new approaches. This results in ideas being put into action. According to learning theory, the team then begins another learning cycle, for as long as it continues along its developmental path.

MUTUALITY PERMITS ASSIMILATION OF OTHER IDEA SYSTEMS

There are other rich sources of ideas about team dynamics. A powerful recent example is the inspiring ideas of systems thinking popularized by Peter Senge in *The Fifth Discipline*. Here the mutuality principle makes it possible for teams to come to terms with what otherwise might be seen as competing systems of thought. We do not have to consider whether systems thinking is 'better than' creative team approaches. We can seek out ways in which the ideas from systems theory can add to, and modify, our existing store of techniques, strategies and structures. An example from real life can be found in the case of the puzzled practitioner (see page 25).

Techniques for vision-building

Techniques for vision-building have to be recognized as succeeding only if they are part of a leadership effort that is supporting change on the other key factors for team success. However, efforts to promote more visual thinking can help directly in several of the factors such as climate, platform of understanding, ownership of ideas and experiential learning. This is why they merit attention.

VISUALIZATION TRAINING

As with almost all techniques for creative development, this approach requires preparation. Untrained teams sometimes operate in a climate in which images flow in plentiful fashion. More typically, the untrained team engaged on a task has a norm of interaction that is dominated by 'rational' behaviours. The preparatory training requires that the team breaks these norms in a psychologically safe situation.

The basis for the approach has been worked out in various team development exercises. It helps if the environment is both supportive and yet distant from the team's normal working conditions. This is one of the justifications for 'away days'.

The leader should have some skills in encouraging people to relax and express personally held views that the norms of behaviour have previously suppressed. As the team 'unfreezes', its members are more able to draw upon vivid personal impressions, and share them.

THE CASE OF THE PUZZLED PRACTITIONER

Gareth contacted us some years ago in his role as head of a large training establishment. Before that, he had been general manager of a sizeable workforce. He was later to become a highly respected director of an overseas task force on behalf of the United Nations.

His colleagues know Gareth as an innovator and as a skilful catalyst of change. He liked nothing better than importing ideas and techniques into his organization. In his training role he was able to turn the training division into a learning laboratory. Within a few months of contacting us, he had arranged a few demonstrations of creative teamwork and had read all the materials we had suggested.

As the training progressed, his nominated colleagues responded positively to the ideas of creative leadership, but Gareth seemed to become more abstracted and lost in his own thoughts.

We found out that he had simultaneously been experimenting with a wide range of systems of team development, problem-solving and systems analysis. In one discussion session Gareth confessed he could not see where creative leadership 'fitted' with process consultancy, although he thought there was 'some connection somewhere'. He was also unclear where it connected with 'task and process components' in team development. As he had also been an enthusiastic reader of systems theories, he wondered where facilitation, self-structuring groups and systems thinking fitted into our scheme of things.

There is both a short and a long answer to Gareth's concerns. The simple reply is that attention to the four aspects of creative leadership 'looks after' some of the confusions that emerge from a survey of theories and consultant recipes on team dynamics.

The longer answer is that Gareth will discover deeper explanations by becoming part of a creative learning team and by introducing any additional concepts of interest into its learning process. Thanks to the mutuality principle, the creative team will seek ways of engaging with the additional techniques and concepts. The outcome will be an enhancement of the team's understanding of creativity and of the other team-based systems under consideration.

We start such training by explaining that the purpose of the exercise is to develop team visualization skills. We also add that many people think they can't do this until they try it, after which they find it easy. It is important that the team members are willing to try and do not feel that they are being manipulated. We therefore operate under 'invitation only' rules and will proceed only if the team members agree to try out something new.

For the first exercise we might ask a team member to give a vivid recollection of a successful experience that some of the other team members might also remember. Other members are asked if they can 'see' the story and take it further. This exercise in team story-telling helps demonstrate what happens when people dig into stored visual memories and construct a shared visual picture.

We then move on to exercises that encourage the team to construct images of events that have not actually happened. Once again, the process may be initiated by a contribution from one team member that is then added to by the other members. The team has begun the process of visualization.

TEAM RESISTANCES TO VISUALIZATION

Each standard team has to find its own way of 'busting' its norms and finding unexpected visions for the future. For some team members the process is unappealing, and even uncomfortable. Such reactions set a challenge that calls for supportive efforts on the part of other team members. As a climate of trust is built and a platform of (empathic) understanding established, the more reluctant team members are prepared to join in. At a pace dictated by the resistance of individual members, teams move to a condition of readiness to break through the barriers of standard performance.

Techniques and structures to support team learning

We postpone to the next chapter the core structure (MPIA) for applications within creative teams. Here we concentrate on team-building methods that we 'imported' into our work with creative teams. They are intended to be examples of many such methods known to experienced team trainers and managers. The three examples focus on learning through the self-applied survey-feedback method. In each case an important characteristic of the team is studied for targeting future creative efforts.

Many teams find themselves using self-report inventories although team members sometimes object that the whole process leads to pigeon-holing and serves no useful purpose. We concede that, wrongly used, inventories fail to promote constructive learning experiences. Our suggestion is for these instruments to be applied for a very specific purpose that is explained to the team members and agreed by them. Our purpose is to provide an explanation of poor team behaviours and suggest a vocabulary that helps members build that all-important platform of understanding through recognizing the characteristic individual differences and treating them as strengths to be harnessed.

EXAMPLE 1: UNDERSTANDING INDIVIDUAL DIFFERENCES USING A SELF-REPORT INVENTORY

What we set out to do is find training experiences through which team members realize that they may be underestimating the worth of each other's contributions. The rationale for this has been aptly summed up by one behavioural researcher as a belief that 'What's different is dangerous'. The process exposes the assumptions behind the old ways of thinking and offers a richer understanding of how team differences can be used productively.

We will illustrate our approach using Michael Kirton's internationally-known Kirton's Adaption Innovation measure (KAI). In a typical training session, team members complete the KAI and are then engaged in other team activities. Before returning the inventory to them, we suggest that one important way in which people differ is in their preferred style of dealing with problems and of creating change. In any team the probability is that there will be a mix of styles.

We then explain that one of these is known as an adaptive style in which people favour gradual ways of solving problems. In discussions they will prefer a few well-worked out ideas to large numbers of speculative ones. In particular they will be aware of the various constraints of any situation and stick to the rules. In contrast, other people adopt what is known as an innovative style and will seek to revolutionize rather than modify ideas whenever possible. Furthermore, these members will be less precise and less attentive to detail.

At this stage someone recognizes his or her preferred style. 'I'm an innovator,' Samuel or Samantha might say. Other team members might agree. With or without prompting, one or two other team members nominate their preferred style to further agreement and disagreement. To add a little more juice to the discussion, each member is given back the self-report assessment, at which stage most groups start to direct their own activities as they continue to discuss the style of individual members.

At an appropriate time the trainers bring the discussion round to the issue of team behaviours. To establish pre-existing norms we ask how the more innovative team members might best describe the 'adaptors'. Under these circumstances the replies, although revealing, do not seem to be hurtful: 'Boring . . . predictable . . . uncreative' would be typical comments. Then the adaptors comment on the 'innovators': 'untrustworthy, crazy, impractical, trouble-makers' might be their response.

We then ask for their assessment of teams with an excess of one or other type. Here there is quite a lot of agreement. A team of adaptors is considered likely to be harmonious, but may have trouble coming up with 'breakout' ideas. A team of innovators is generally assumed to have plenty of fun, while being hopelessly unproductive and chaotic.

'What might be the make-up of the most successful teams?' we ask.

'A mix of adaptors and innovators,' is the spontaneous reply.

This is a conclusion to be found in a dozen articles and books on team dynamics. Because the learning occurs in a discovery mode, however, it has a greater chance of becoming integrated into a genuine shift of behaviours and beliefs.

Other important issues can also be pointed out after a team has become introduced to the basic principles of adaption-innovation theory. It provides clear support for the idea that everyone is creative – an assumption essential for effective team-building. Some team members are creative in a more adaptive way. Some are creative in a more innovative way. This is a powerful antidote to the contrary and widespread assumption that all the creative work of a team derives from one or two individuals. Such a view almost certainly confuses creative contribution with innovative style.

EXAMPLE 2: UNDERSTANDING THE GROUP CLIMATE FOR CREATIVITY

One excellent way of drawing attention to the key success factor of climate is to use a creative climate inventory such as that developed by the eminent Swedish researcher, Göran Ekvall. The training process begins with the completion of a short inventory. The feedback is reserved for a subsequent training session after the inventories have been examined and the results compared with those from other teams.

The inventory splits climate into ten factors whose presence differentiates between high-performance and low-performance teams. The factors are:

- Challenge
- Freedom
- Idea support
- Trust
- Dynamism

- Playfulness
- Debates
- Conflicts ('ego clashes')
- Risk-taking
- Idea time.

A team wishing to make the most of their project will discuss each factor in turn.

Challenge

If possible, the project should be planned so that all the interesting assignments do not go to the same people. Teams can deliberately set themselves challenges. During training, ideas can be suggested such as organizing an event of interest, perhaps a site visit, in the middle of the tedium of detailed implementation.

Freedom

A feature of much project management is tight control of budgets and resources which can lead to feelings of constraint and frustration. The team can discuss ways to negotiate or claim some latitude over the way the project is carried out. There are almost always opportunities for this if the team applies its creative efforts to the matter.

Idea support

This climate factor is clearly connected to one of the seven factors differentiating dream teams from others, namely idea ownership. In examining its climate for creativity, a team is advised to discuss the way in which ideas are treated. Is there evidence of mutual support for one another's ideas? If the team feels that ideas are generally treated negatively, it might consider ways of strengthening support for one another's ideas. One of the most powerful and simple ways of doing this is through the deliberate application of the Yes And technique, which will be described in the next section.

Trust

In some climates, information is seen as an important bargaining chip to corporate success. If it is withheld, there is likely to be little trust among team members. A start can be made if teams discuss the issue and acknowledge evidence from shared behaviours. It may become clear that devious or secretive behaviours are 'accidentally' rewarded – an unintended consequence of personal reward systems, for example. The creativity required for solving problems then has to be augmented by creativity directed towards finding new team structures that reward collaborative team work.

Dynamism

We all know what it is like to work in an atmosphere where nothing seems to move and everything is just too much trouble. Similarly, there are invariably times in a project when progress seems slow or non-existent. This can sap a team's energy. It is very tiring to work with people who can't see the point of what you are doing and who seem to raise objections all the time. An indirect way to explore this is to hold a team discussion at which the current platform of understanding is frankly examined to include those frustrations and possible steps to manage them.

Most teams find they know one or two people who can play an energizing role based on their general team disposition. 'How can we get them involved?' is a good starting question. Look for people who seem lively and energetic, and who have achieved things themselves. Success breeds success and lively colleagues will help you through mid-project blues.

Playfulness

The capacity to see humorous aspects of a situation can certainly help to keep a project moving. It can be damaging if a team takes itself too seriously, perhaps because there is too great a respect for status or position. This is one of those features that call for leadership and a willingness on the part of more senior people to find ways of lightening up the climate. Humour during idea generation nearly always indicates that a good climate has been achieved.

It should be noted, however, that there are very different views of what constitutes humour. What works in a male locker-room may puzzle or offend in a mixed gender team.

Debates

It is unlikely that committed individuals from different backgrounds will always agree with each other. There will often be heated debates about key decisions and it is important for the health of the project that time is allowed for this. Open, honest opinions can lead to a constructive resolution of the situation. In any event, it is vital to concentrate on the subject matter and not permit the arguments to stray on to personal grievances. We distinguish between debates and conflicts. Debates occur when team members are comfortable enough with one another to be open about differing views. The differences are explored in a spirit of seeking the best outcome, regardless of who suggested it.

Conflicts

Differences that are not managed constructively produce conflicts rather than debates. There is an extensive body of knowledge about dealing with conflicts. No one needs reminding that personal grudges are widespread and sometimes seem to be directed towards quite trivial issues. Conflicts are exacerbated when the protagonists remain fixated on a single point of view. Our experience is that teams can develop the skills to deal with conflicts, based on the creative principle of seeking changes that respect the needs of all parties. Conflict resolution is another area in which the mutuality principle is needed for win-win outcomes.

Teams from hell never seem to escape the conflicts that flare up among team members. Standard teams and even a few dream teams tolerate conflicts in the short term if there is a wider goal to which they can give temporary priority.

Risk-taking

Applying a novel solution to a problem always involves an element of risk. It helps if the team can clarify what the boundaries of their project are and how much leeway they are likely to have. Pilot schemes and trial products can help to clarify the risks involved. A team that is totally averse to risks is unlikely to achieve even modest conceptual breakthroughs while successful entrepreneurs survive in inherently risky environments.

Team members are likely to have different thresholds of acceptable risk, however, and the team-building process assists in managing this variety. Many organizations have developed comprehensive risk-management systems, although these tend to stop short of addressing the all-important aspect of perceived personal or psychological feelings of risk experienced in some situations. The creative climate is one in which there is no shame attached to revealing such personal fears. Discussing these matters builds a supportive platform of understanding.

Idea time

Successful teams seem to make time to explore ideas thoroughly before they move forward. They realize that idea generation involves different types of behaviour and do their best to manage their schedules accordingly. One of the most frequent cries in any modern organization is 'We haven't got time!' If a team is to be creatively successful, it needs to nurture its precious idea time. The pressures are compounded where there is an unresolved sense

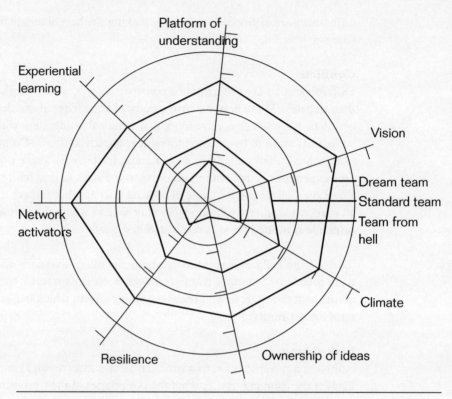

Figure 2.5 Team diagnostic with typical profiles for dream teams, standard teams and teams from hell

that some behaviours are time-wasting. We have seen teams gradually (and sometime rapidly) reach the conclusion that much so-called productive time is essentially wasted in activity that leads nowhere. They also find that, paradoxically, 'time-outs', 'away days' and 'meditative breaks' are not wasted but yield the most valuable longer-term benefits.

EXAMPLE 3: DREAM TEAM DIAGNOSTIC

We have recently been experimenting with a team diagnostic and an extension to our work with the creative climate inventory which is based on the seven factors of successful teams. The seven factors are assessed on a diagnostic chart shown in Figure 2.5. The chart has seven lines radiating like spokes from a bicycle wheel, with each spoke representing one of the seven factors. When the team assessments for the factors are placed on the chart, and then joined up, a seven-sided figure (a heptagon) is produced. The greater the area of the heptagon produced, the more highly the team has been rated. The heptagon for any team can be benchmarked against those of a team from hell (the inner heptagon); a standard team (middle heptagon); and a dream team (outer heptagon). Any factor for which a team is assessed particularly poorly can easily be identified.

It is important for teams to use the diagnostic as a means of focusing discussion towards team development. Otherwise the exercise reinforces the team's belief in its prevailing climate, rather than encouraging discussion on how to improve on the climate.

THE YES AND TECHNIQUE

The Yes And technique is one of the simplest and most powerful ways of building teams and at the same time building ideas. The technique helps individuals and teams to avoid the either-or trap of rejecting ideas which could be turned into winners with a little more effort. Dream teams use Yes And automatically; in contrast, teams from hell are unable to feel comfortable with its use.

The basic elements of the technique are as follows. A team is showing signs of either-or thinking. The leader (or some other team member) finds a way of drawing attention to the negativity, using the expression Yes And. The expression is sufficiently unusual to help team members break out of the kind of negative mind-set that produces Yes But reactions.

A powerful Yes And takes an idea and exposes the aspect that has received the most hostile criticism in a way that invites the team to overcome the weakness. The either-or reaction effectively says 'That's a bad idea. Let's kill it.' The Yes And technique effectively says 'That's an idea with a weakness. Let's see if the weakness can be overcome.'

Often the approach rescues potentially valuable ideas. Equally important, the team that works in this way develops positive mind-sets that eventually become automatic. In the following examples, the team leaders are role models for anyone interested in creative leadership. They work hard at overcoming Yes Buts and developing Yes And ideas.

Mutuality in action

The marketing manager of a hotel and leisure group was looking for ways to exploit the new opportunities to conduct marriages outside a church or register office setting. At a meeting of one of their subsidiary companies, a group of motorway service stations, he suggested that selected stations apply for licences to conduct weddings. After the howls of laughter died down, there was a barrage of objections.

> I can see it now; the wedding parties getting mixed up with the football coaches!
>
> What's the bride going to do – queue up for an all day breakfast? She'll get grease on her dress!
>
> Perhaps we could get the petrol companies to put pink neon hearts on the petrol station!

The manager had mentally prepared himself for these reactions. He knew the habitual behaviours in his team meetings and had already thought through some of the objections. As the comments were made, he jotted the points down on a whiteboard. After the jokes had subsided he developed the idea, picking off the objections.

> The idea is quite novel, so we'd have to make sure that we signposted things clearly. It might give us the opportunity to build a separate facility, connected to our motels by a walkway. That would make sure there was no need to take photographs in the rain. Weddings at weekends could boost our motel bookings. We could offer a package including overnight accommodation. That would bring the occupancy up; weekends are our quiet period.
>
> One advantage of our locations is that they are easy to find and we could have designated parking. Register offices tend to be in town centres and parking is impossible. How many people here have missed the actual ceremony because they can't find the

church? Most people can find our main
service stations. I was looking at
population trends and realized that many
remarriages have at least one partner
falling into the WOSTA category
(financially 'Wiped Out. Second Time
Around'). They are older people, often
with demanding jobs. We could offer a
package, including reception, cake,
accommodation. We could even arrange for
one of our managers to be licensed as a
registrar.

I know we'd have to work on the decor to
create the right impression. Maybe we could
make a case for someone to go to Las Vegas
to look at the wedding chapels and learn
from the way they do things there.

Perhaps because of his creative way of turning objections to opportunities,
the other members began to warm to the idea. Or, as the manager wondered
later, maybe they had become rather interested in an all-expenses paid trip
to Las Vegas.

The manager was setting a positive example and acting as a role model. He
persisted in similar mode, and in time the team gradually became more open
to new ideas. The first negative reactions may have come from the
preconception that weddings mean white dresses, bells and confetti. The
prevailing assumptions of what happened at service stations was so different
it restricted the possibility of any new idea – without some effort at Yes
Anding.

In our second example, the team received support through a leadership style
that encouraged more involvement in Yes Anding. The context was that of a
regular meeting of an amenities committee of a large organization. In
previous meetings the team had behaved not unlike that in the first example.
As a consequence, the team leader, Penny, had proposed a few simple rules
to deal with negativity. She suggested that the members had previously
treated ideas as if they were clay pigeons, too easily shot down. Her
colleagues reacted jokingly to her cartoon shown in Figure 2.6. Penny
persisted by suggesting that maybe they thought of themselves more like
James Bond with a licence to kill ideas. She was asking them to take out a
licence to create as shown in Figure 2.7.

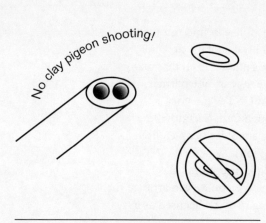

Figure 2.6   No clay pigeon shooting!

The single item on the agenda was doorstep smoking. In many countries, the impact of smoking on health has been recognized and legislation has been introduced to protect non-smokers from the consequences of passive smoking. Many organizations now insist that smoking does not take place in the workplace environment, leading to the phenomenon of the 'doorstep smoker'. Even in atrocious weather in the middle of winter you can see groups of individuals huddled at building entrances, smoking their cigarettes. There is often no provision made for the discarded cigarette ends, which are thrown to the ground to gather in soggy, depressing-looking heaps.

Penny, as meeting chairperson, outlined the situation as it affected their own organization and there was general agreement about the platform of understanding. The buildings and estate manager than spoke up. 'I've asked Terry to look into the possibility of providing decorative stone ashtrays outside the building to try to stop the litter.'

She had barely had time to complete her proposal before the objections began. 'Yes but, if they are a nice design, people will steal them . . . But in wet weather they will look horrible.' Penny stood up and switched on the overhead projector showing the warning against clay pigeon shooting. The team members began to laugh.

'I suppose we could make them with a very heavy base,' the first objector admitted.

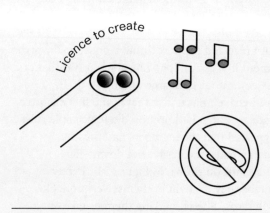

Figure 2.7   Licence to create

'Yes and we could attach them to the wall, so they would be less likely to disappear . . .' Penny added.

One team member commented that they could be designed to be invisible. Another remained unconvinced: 'But surely that will look as if we are condoning smoking.'

By now, however, the momentum had gathered towards team positivity. 'That is a possibility, and to get round that we could print the government health warning on them . . .' someone said.

At the end of the meeting they had constructed a demonstration model out of bits of paper and paperclips and one of the team members undertook to cost out the design for their next meeting. A few months later the design won an award and was adapted in various countries by the parent organization.

The creative leadership style

There is a place where the creative leadership style exists in a form that can be easily studied. We recommend it as somewhere which all students of creative leadership need to visit. The place is wherever the so-called structured techniques for creative problem-solving in teams are practised.

The role is that required of a person leading the idea generation. For technical reasons it may be split into a 'team recorder' and a 'facilitator'. Put together these roles and you have the essence of creative leadership. Its most important and unusual feature is that the creative leader is essential for the ideas to flow. Yet the leader contributes to that process by putting the ideas of the team members before his or her own ideas. The style is one in which the leader is also the servant to the task of ensuring the flow of the team's ideas.

The learning engendered is summarized well by Sarah, a project manager who had completed a training programme as a creative leader. In her personal learning log she noted that:

> As I have become more experienced in stimulating the creativity of others I have become aware of pitfalls that hinder a creative style. I remember in a previous job I was charged with setting up a cross-functional unit. We had a lot of freedom to define our mission, goals, values and processes. I could always see lots of possibilities and I thought it would help if I threw in numerous ideas. I was rather hurt to learn that I was seen as somewhat dominating by team members who felt there was little point to contributing themselves. This is an important lesson. It's more important you keep things moving and encourage the others, making the whole thing as enjoyable as you can.

Another experienced creative leader summed up his learning as follows:

> It's as if creativity is 'by invitation only'. You
> can only invite a team to try some new
> approach or even to go along with the plan
> of a meeting.

What did he mean? Mainly, that creative leadership operates by opening up possibilities and gaining the acceptance and trust of the team in the process. We have seen that invitational style frequently in the most skilled creative leaders. It may sound 'soft' and laissez-faire. Indeed, the creative leader who follows the invitational style puts himself or herself at the mercy of the team is an example of 'flying blind'. But it works. Those leaders who trust their teams in this way have fewer 'leadership battles' than those with more traditional 'direct and control styles'. That is not to say there will never be storms. The form-storm-norm-perform model is right on that point. The invitational style can build one part of a platform of understanding that may ride out the storm, and even help calm the waters considerably for plainer sailing in future.

Too often, the pressures of day-to-day operation reduce the scope for experimenting with a creative leadership style. That is one of the most powerful arguments for setting time aside for such productive trials. In the next chapter we shall look at one approach specifically designed to support creativity and learning, so that the team enhances its chances of going beyond the standard performance to exceptional and sustained performance levels.

Summary

This chapter has concentrated on creative leadership and its consequences. Creative leaders demonstrate a strong belief in win-win outcomes (mutuality); an empowering and motivating style; strategies that encourage sensitivity and learning; and a sensitivity to the balance between individual and team needs.

Researchers Collins and Porras discovered what they termed 'the genius of the and' in successful visionary companies. Encouraging behaviours which avoid either-or thinking, supporting learning through experience and assimilating different ideas systems are ways to encourage the mutuality principle. The behaviour creative leaders encourage can be exemplified by the phrase 'There must be other ways . . . There might be better ways.'

Creative visualization is needed for teams to escape from the norms of standard performance. However, such efforts can only succeed in conjunction with other key factors which encourage team members to become more open to sharing their individual beliefs and images.

The use of self-report inventories to build team profiles, a deeper understanding of what influences a creative climate and discussion stimulated by the dream team diagnostic are all approaches to support creative leadership.

Creative leaders help the team develop their ideas, setting a climate for creativity by encouraging trust and openness. This should not be confused with a laissez-faire approach. Frequently it requires leadership to put the ideas of the team before those of the leader. Teams cannot be ordered to be positive. As one experienced leader put it, 'Creativity is by invitation only.'

3 ENHANCING TEAM CREATIVITY: THE MPIA SYSTEM

When all else fails . . .

We were flattered to be invited to a reception as guests of an award-winning project team we had worked with. We had spent some time coaching the team in our 'full-blown' model for creative teamwork, the MPIA system. After the meal, the project leader rose to review the events leading up to the award.

> We would like to thank our corporate sponsor for the faith placed in us. It was a new experience, thrown in at the deep end to go overseas with a blank piece of paper to assess the market for . . . (a well-known medical product). The whole experience has been fantastic, but now that you have been kind enough to recognize our efforts, my team wanted me to set the record straight. You might think it was all plain sailing, using those techniques we were trained in. Well, it didn't work like that. We had three weeks to prepare for the trip. Most of that time we didn't know what to do. We dug out all the data. We worked through all the figures and contacts you gave us. In the end we were in meetings 18 hours a day. We were going round in circles. Anyway, that last weekend before we went away somebody said 'It's no good – we've tried everything else. We could try that MPIA creativity stuff.' So we did. (*Laughter from the rest of the team.*) And it worked. So we want to say to any teams listening: 'Don't do what we did if you get a new project. Don't wait until it's nearly too late for creativity or anything else to save

you. You may think it's all a bit weird. I
suppose we did. But it's not. Don't wait
until you are nearly in the jungle before you
start.

DEVELOP THE CREATIVITY HABIT EARLY

Here is the paradox in efforts to break free from the norms of behaviour.
The prize-winning team members had stuck to the familiar long after they
might have 'tried some creativity stuff'. Faced with an exciting new project
they saw no reason to depart from tried and tested ways of operating until it
was almost too late. This is an extreme example of a very common pattern
of behaviour. It is one of the reasons we urge teams to acquire the creativity
habit early.

The habit is one that can be developed by experimenting with a structure
through which the norms of 'ordinary' behaviour are more easily challenged
– as was recognized, almost too late, by the team described above.

The MPIA system as a learning aid

In this chapter we consider the basic principles of team creativity, as the
essential differentiating feature of dream teams. We then introduce the
MPIA system of studying and influencing team creativity. MPIA stands for
Mapping, Perspectives, and Ideas in Action. The approach is one that we
have worked with and refined over many years and we will explain it further
in subsequent chapters. It operates so that, regardless of circumstances, the
team can apply it in some way or another to develop creative skills and, as a
consequence, produce more effective ideas.

There is a vital difference between the MPIA system and the creative
problem-solving structures from which it evolved. Earlier and related
systems for stimulating creativity emphasized ways of developing new ideas.
But in stressing the importance of breaking mental barriers, they overlooked
the role of the learning processes needed for teams to transcend those
barriers. MPIA is designed for use as a coherent learning system, within
which both team learning and creative ideas are more easily fostered.

A creativity refresher

Creativity is a term that can trigger strong emotions. It is associated with mad scientists, artistic genius and a range of craft activities from basket-weaving to body-painting. We persist with the term, because we need some way of describing the processes of discovery, and because attempts to replace the concept with other less controversial words seem unsatisfactory. This section covers aspects of creativity that will be referred to later on in the text. In it we show how creativity can be understood in a way that helps clear up the commonest confusions and objections. For readers unfamiliar with the notions of creative problem-solving, this section is important as an overview of key ideas in the rest of the book.

DEFINING CREATIVITY

There are many definitions of creativity. For our purpose we suggest

Creativity = novelty + added value

The implication is that creativity is a process that is judged within a specific context. The novelty is that which makes a difference to those most directly concerned with the process. Thus a team that overlooks an obvious possibility is creative in discovering what has been overlooked.

Under this definition there is no difficulty in accepting that we all have the capacity to be more creative, and that this creativity can be applied to our work environment. Some working conditions are more constraining than others. However, it is a rare situation that will not benefit from the application of creative problem-solving. You will notice that in our equation, novelty is not enough; to be creative in a work context you need ideas that are actionable and relevant to the situation.

Mind-sets

Our approach draws on a theory of human information processing influenced by mental blinkers which we describe as mind-sets. On a basis of general mind-set theory we can demonstrate the need to break out of exclusively analytical thinking within problems treated as closed. The result is a shift towards what has become known as systems thinking.

We make sense of the world around us by filtering information into patterns that we can recognize quickly. Such filters make us over-sensitive to factors

BOILED FROGS, MIND-SET AND CREATIVE JOLTS

Business guru Charles Handy has written vividly of the boiled frog syndrome. This metaphor of the human condition suggests that a frog remains calm if placed in a bowl of water of comfortable temperature. Furthermore, it is unconcerned as the temperature is gradually raised. Eventually the frog is boiled. In contrast, a frog dropped into hot water makes every effort to jump out. This unpleasant metaphor may be taken to illustrate how human mind-sets may resist gradual threats, whereas a sudden jolt may serve to awaken us to danger.

Mental jolts can be deliberately induced. Exposure to a creativity technique may serve as an unexpected jolt, as the climate is substantially different from our habitual one made comfortable through conditioning and mind-sets. Some creativity techniques of the lateral-thinking variety are based on specific procedures for increasing the 'voltage' of the jolt.

we think relevant, often at the expense of other useful pieces of information. This over-sensitivity can be labelled as a 'mind-set' which is derived from the four Es: experience, education, expertise and expectations. Mind-sets sensitize us to some important things, and often serve us well. It helps to be sensitized to potential danger, for instance; a flashing red light indicates to most people that they should be on their guard, and ready to act. In other words, it triggers a swift response. Many standard safety procedures are carried out on the automatic pilot of a person's mind-set. Thus learning from experience is eventually converted into conditioning factors that influence our unthinking actions. This happens at work, and in many of life's routines such as getting ready to go out in the morning, playing a sport, driving a car or doing crossword puzzles.

In unfamiliar circumstances mind-sets have their disadvantages. We may stay on automatic pilot. It may well be that there is a psychological defence mechanism at play. Actions under the control of mind-sets are reassuring – the world has no unexpected threats in store for us and we are receiving no warning signals of change. Indeed, this deceptively comfortable state persists until we are jolted painfully into accepting that something has changed.

This can happen especially when a multi-disciplinary team tackles a problem and different mind-sets are brought to bear on the issue. Instead of being able to accommodate diverse views, individuals fight each other: 'I am right so any other view must be wrong.'

We cannot eliminate mind-sets, nor should we want to. In many circumstances they play a simplifying role, protecting us from information overload and permitting 'unconsciously expert' behaviours to flow from them. Although they function at a below-conscious level, we can learn to become more aware of them. Under stress they may take over, reducing the contribution to our actions from conscious thinking. The general tendency is to concentrate for a while, then to lose concentration as the old mind-sets reassent themselves.

This approach to mind-sets presumes that an escape requires some shock or jolt. We suggest that the process is not one that is susceptible to an appeal to reason. Furthermore, we always see another's mind-sets much more clearly than we see our own! Creative problem-solving techniques help us become more aware of our mind-sets and give us tools to help us challenge them.

Whole-brain thinking, and its significance for sustaining the mutuality principle

There is evidence to show that there are two patterns of problem-solving behaviour, which have become known as left-brain and right-brain thinking. Left-brain thinking is a popular shorthand way of describing thinking which expresses itself in logical, step-by-step and structured ways. In contrast, right-brain thinking is intuitive and takes unexpected leaps that challenge the constraints and boundaries of left-brain brain thinking.

Most courses on creativity, including our own, touch on left-brain and right-brain styles of thinking. Some of the teaching, in our view, has unfortunate unintended consequences. Instead of serving to illustrate an important opportunity for creative team development, it accidentally belittles the majority of people as uncreative left-brainers. We find this quite unnecessary and, indeed, at odds with the fundamental principle of mutuality for creative leadership. The main need for addressing left-brain and right-brain bias in teams is to avoid the temptation to reject the opposing style (a similar difficulty was encountered and dealt with in the diagnosis of adaptors and innovators in Chapter 2). Discussion can build a platform of understanding for capitalising on these individual differences. Indeed, a team has to be encouraged to move towards the Both And attitude here, as in many other ways, as a recognition of the mutuality principle.

In our own treatment of left-right brain biases, we suggest that creativity-enhancing techniques deliberately stretch team members away from their habitual styles of thinking. Those participants with a left-brain bias are

THE RELATIONSHIP BETWEEN CREATIVE BEHAVIOUR AND LEFT-BRAIN AND RIGHT-BRAIN THINKING STYLE

Conventional education tends to emphasize the value of left-brain thinking, especially in professional occupations such as engineering, accounting and computer programming. Conversely we have found many individuals whose jobs are in the leisure, entertainment and 'people-centred' professions whose bias is towards right-brain thinking.

Most managerial tasks require skills in both left- and right-brain modes of thought. Particularly at general management levels, problems reflecting high levels of uncertainty may need right-brain intuitive processes during decision-making. Creativity is a combination of left-brain attention to facts and logic and right-brain receptivity to 'seeing the whole picture'.

encouraged to 'go with the flow' when the more right-brain techniques are in use. Similarly, those of right-brain bias have to become more accepting of the need for accurate analysis or left-brain techniques when this is required.

The capacity to find shared visions almost certainly requires most teams to come to terms with predominantly left-brain biases, and become more open to mental pictures of desired future states. These issues come into play with the metaphoric options for stimulating creativity discussed below.

OPEN AND CLOSED PROBLEMS

Strictly speaking, we make sense of our world by creating boundaries within which we choose to operate. The influential theorist and Nobel-prize winner Herbert Simon calls this the process of 'bounded rationality'. In less formal terms, we can regard many of the issues we deal with as relatively closed. By that we mean that the boundaries and constraints of the situation remain fixed, and that the process is marked by the predictability of the ultimate solution. The application of our learned (and hard-earned) expertise and experience will frequently lead to a satisfactory resolution, with few unintended consequences. It is also apparent where the responsibility for dealing with the issue lies. There is a clear 'problem owner' with the resources to make something happen.

In contrast, complex project briefs required for the launching of a new product, or the implementation of a new computing system may involve a great deal of uncertainty. Boundaries and constraints will undoubtedly change during the project and novel and unexpected ideas may be needed. In many cases it will be impossible to prove that a suggested course of action will work until it is tried in practice. More often than not, 'solutions' will have knock-on effects and unintended consequences. Accepting that you are dealing with an open-ended situation, and employing the creative team approaches suggested in this book, can lead to more harmonious teamwork and more productive outputs.

Approaches to boost creativity: (1) the metaphoric option

The assumptions of a standard team are, as we have argued, self-reinforcing. One of the most interesting approaches for breaking the assumptions involves the deliberate practice of metaphoric thinking.

MAKING THE FAMILIAR STRANGE AND THE STRANGE FAMILIAR

This principle can be directed towards breaking conventional assumptions and ideas that contribute towards the glass ceiling effect that holds back team progress.

An example of this occurred in a large company that was in the process of merging two quite different financial services businesses. Teams of highly successful merchant bankers and options traders had been thrown together and each had to propose a medium-term strategic plan. During a painful meeting at their new common headquarters, most of the teams seemed to have accepted their fate with little enthusiasm. In their 'breakout' rooms the teams seemed to have exhausted their energies in personal 'storming'. The norm was one of preserving into the future as much of their past culture as they possibly could. One of the bankers had pointedly brought his own silver tray and tea service rather than use the plastic cups from the vending machines.

At a plenary session to report progress, the evidence was clear. The teams had no clear ideas except 'business as usual'. One of the facilitators asked if it would help for them to hear her view.

> You all seem to be suffering. The board has asked you to plan for smooth implementation of the merger. Don't worry about that for the moment. I've got this picture that you've been in a storm and there's been a shipwreck. One ship has gone down, and now somehow the survivors are all in one ship.

After the laughter had subsided there were more jokes about who was on the menu for lunch. Then some animated discussions began. They had begun to see how the 'strange' idea of a shipwreck had forced them past the assumptions and into new ideas for the future. The strange had been connected to the familiar. Throughout the retreat, the metaphor continued to serve as a spur to new thinking, and as a means of shifting attention away from the repetitive discussions of the previous sessions.

PERSONAL ANALOGY ('HOW WOULD YOU FEEL IF?')

An amenities team had to formulate a plan for redeveloping a disused stretch of canal situated in a place of unspoiled natural beauty and close to a rural settlement. The team had been provided with a highly detailed consultancy report. They were not convinced by the recommendation of the consultants that seemed to risk opposition from all the involved constituencies.

These 'stakeholders' were not involved in the initial discussions. However, the team were able to stretch their own thinking by imagining how the stakeholders might feel. The team members allotted themselves roles. One became a local councillor. Another was the representative of the canal society. A third was a National Trust executive. Yet another was a countryside planner. Finally there was a householder. A team leader acted as a mediator (hoping to encourage Yes And thinking).

Having previously struggled with ideas, the team now found that the process opened a floodgate of suggestions. Members were quickly able to find alternatives to the consultants' ideas that were more consistent with local concerns. Later, when they did meet the stakeholders, they were able to express their ideas with considerable empathy. The metaphoric exercise had created new ideas and indirectly helped the team members to work as network activators.

IMAGINIZATION

In his book of the same name, Gareth Morgan describes imaginization as the art of creative management. He suggests that the images we hold of organizations have to be replaced. Instead of seeing them as machines or pyramids, we should think of them as spider plants capable of spinning many individual daughter plants.

Imaginization appears to be a form of metaphoric thinking in which the metaphors have been carefully selected for their potency and are powerful enough to become the theme for a metaphoric discussion. As Morgan indicates, the next step in a team's development occurs when it wants to 'fly solo' and create its own images. We agree, although we would commend the writings of Morgan for those team leaders who have become interested in metaphoric excursions.

Approaches to boost creativity: (2) the lateral option

We now touch on another group of techniques that can be seen as general mind-set busters. While various practitioners such as ourselves might claim to have developed innovative blockbusting techniques, the field is dominated by the techniques of Edward de Bono under the rubric of lateral thinking approaches. We therefore refer to blockbusting techniques as the lateral thinking option, in recognition of his contribution in this area.

Edward de Bono has described typical problem-solving as 'digging a hole deeper', when there may be a need 'to dig a hole in some other place'. When digging deeply we are under the control of our mind-sets. We search for solutions close to our past experience. Where else? When we are unsuccessful, we put more and more effort into searching close to those areas most familiar to us. Progress can only be made if some jolt occurs. If the jolt does not come naturally, we have to contrive it for ourselves.

Lateral thinking is not an intellectual trick. It is a skill that can be developed through regular practice and with a willingness to try something different. In teamwork it can help to add momentum when progress seems slow. We now describe three blockbusting approaches that have served us well in our work with creative teams.

REVERSALS

When 'stuck' with a problem it can often help to 'turn our thinking upside down'. It may be discovered that the 'obvious' approach – or sequence of steps – can be usefully reversed. In this way a threat may become an opportunity. With practice it may become apparent that there are several ways of switching your thinking, each of which is a kind of reversal. This can help the team become more positive about potential drawbacks. A famous example of this is the development of the 3M Post-it® Note, which arose out of the search to find a use for glue which would not stick permanently.

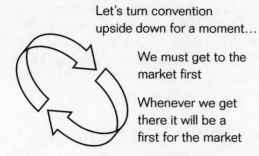

Let's turn convention
upside down for a moment...

We must get to the
market first

Whenever we get
there it will be a
first for the market

Figure 3.1 The reversals invitation

Several valuable ideas have emerged in our work when team members have been challenged to 'try some reversed thinking'. A difficult engineering problem was solved when a piece of equipment was pulled into place instead of being pushed. Pilferage of experimental product samples was not reduced but allowed to proceed – and the results proved to be a crude measure of product sales potential. Figure 3.1 shows the principle in action.

THE INTERMEDIATE IMPOSSIBLE ('WOULDN'T IT BE WONDERFUL IF . . . ?')

This concept encourages team members to dream about a future in which their ideal solution to a problem comes about. Some people find it difficult

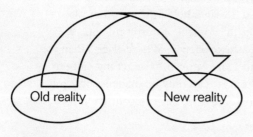

Old reality

New reality

Wouldn't it be wonderful if...
roads could renew their surfaces like skin?

Figure 3.2 The 'Wouldn't it be wonderful if . . . ?' invitation

to escape from everyday reality and the 'intermediate impossible' can be immensely helpful in this respect. Visualizing a fanciful or fantastic idea can be the spur to taking a new direction. Akio Morita, the founder of Sony and the inventor of the Sony Walkman, dreamt that everyone could carry their music with them. This spurred him on to the development of one of the most influential pieces of audio-equipment ever invented.

Figure 3.2 shows the basic principle. In teams the invitation may take the expression 'Wouldn't it be wonderful if . . . ?'

RANDOM JUXTAPOSITION

Sometimes momentum is lost if the realities and complexities of a project bog down a team. Impetus can be regained from the energy generated by a random stimulus. This may be a word that forces the team to make fresh associations about the subject in question. The stimulus may not provide ideas directly, but it gives new direction and interest to the process, as shown in Figure 3.3.

One of the simpler ways of providing a jolt is to say something provocative simply to promote a shift of attention in the meeting. Some managers will

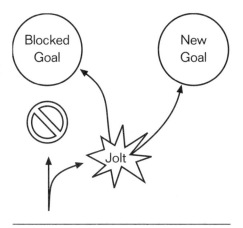

Figure 3.3   The jolt that triggers insights

confess to deliberately employing this approach, talking about causing a diversion or even 'rolling in a hand grenade'.

We often challenge a team to find new directions of thought by picking a word at random from a copy of the morning newspaper, or a dictionary. In Chapter 5 we supply a set of words that have proved particularly effective.

Our own preference has been to build up a great deal of experience with a few techniques that continue to serve us well. Readers will find numerous other techniques for busting mind-sets in books by Edward de Bono, Andy Van Gundy and many others. The methods are fun to experiment with, and we are in no way suggesting they are inferior to those that have evolved as favourites within the specific circumstances of our work.

Introduction to the MPIA system for supporting team creativity

We consider that the principles already outlined go a long way to helping teams achieve better self-awareness and improved creative performance. However, for teams wishing to take a more serious approach to their potential for creativity, an integrated system is called for. We have developed MPIA from a combination of practice and study of existing creative problem-solving systems. We will first offer an orientation to the system so that some expectations can be set. We will then outline MPIA first in its most simple format, and subsequently adding what is needed for more advanced applications. Each of the three chapters in Part II deal with one of the three broad areas of creative thinking and learning dealt with within the MPIA system.

ORIENTATION

Before reading any further, the reader who enjoys a mental challenge might like to reflect on the two questions in Figure 3.4. The information that forms the basis of an answer has been already given towards the beginning of this chapter. The first question is 'What kinds of systems do you believe were the

Orientation question 1: Which creativity-spurring systems were influences in the development of the MPIA system?

Orientation question 2: What is the vital difference between the MPIA system, and those creativity-spurring systems from which it developed?

Figure 3.4   The orientation questions for introducing the MPIA system to new users

ones that influenced us during the development of the MPIA approach?' The second question is 'What makes the MPIA system different from these earlier systems?'

If you cannot attempt the orientation questions we suggest you go back to the beginning of this chapter. There we indicated that the MPIA system evolved from the so-called structured techniques for stimulating creativity. Perhaps the most obvious influence was the Parnes-Osborn creative problem-solving model. We were also influenced by the blockbusting techniques of lateral thinking. If you remembered some of these points, you are well oriented regarding the origins of the MPIA system.

The vital difference is that we have also been influenced by the principles of learning theory. In some of our earliest work in the 1970s we referred to the learning approach as creative analysis – or the study of creative experiences to enhance future creative behaviours. This component in our work is not emphasized in the creativity literature. Whereas the structured creativity techniques are, first and foremost, idea-enabling techniques, MPIA is both this and a learning system. Indeed it has special aspects as a learning system such as the mutuality principle through which the team can examine earlier training and beliefs and strengthen future procedures.

TAKING CREATIVITY SERIOUSLY

In our training we find that, unless we are careful, the participants take a long time to realize the importance of MPIA as a learning aid. The dominant mind-set is that MPIA is just another creativity technique that is going to provide new ideas. That is why we challenged expectations in the orientation exercise. It may have demonstrated something about your *own* expectations.

We emphasize this point because applying creativity techniques has remained rather a minority pursuit in business circles. A relatively small number of users find them valuable, but they have never persuaded a broader constituency to take their results seriously. If MPIA continues to be perceived as 'just another creativity technique', it is likely to be treated in the same way. If you always do what you've always done, you'll always get what you've always got.

THE MPIA STAGES

At the start of courses on creativity in teams we give out a small card to which participants refer throughout the programme. We know it is useful because we have met people several years later who show us the card, which they keep close to hand as a valued support to their thinking.

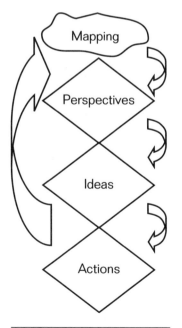

As inevitable in a learning system, it has gone through several developments. Our current card contains a representation of the MPIA approach as shown in Figure 3.5.

This shows a flow chart of four stages, in which the M stands for mapping, the P for perspectives, the I for ideas, and the A for actions. It is the version that has recently been made available for use in all UK business schools through Government Research Council support.

By presenting the system as four stages, the card conveys the impression of a step-by-step process. There are good reasons for first learning the system in this fashion. For example, it is easier to connect up the overall sequence with other well-known schemes for studying problem-solving, including the Parnes-Osborn model already discussed, which is better known in the US.

In the chapters on creative teams in practice in Part II of this book, we also work with a version of MPIA that reminds us that it is a learning process. A circular motif is used for this

Figure 3.5   The MPIA structure in linear form

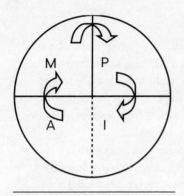

Figure 3.6 The MPIA approach in cyclical form

as shown in Figure 3.6. Just as experiential learning is believed to move in a development cycle, so can application of the MPIA help in a continued development of our mental maps. For the moment however, we will consider the simple business card version.

THE CREATIVE DIAMOND

In the simple business card version, three of the stages are represented as diamond shapes. This is a very common symbol which has been used in creative problem-solving systems since the early work of Alex Osborn and Sid Parnes. It reminds users that creative behaviours require two components. The first component is that of divergence or opening up possibilities, the second of making selections or decisions.

In Osborn's brainstorming, there was a single diamond of idea generation and selection. The technique provided rules originally stated as 'postponing judgement, hitch-hiking and freewheeling'. These principles can be seen as ways of setting a creative (Yes And) climate. Other techniques are required to help in the decision-making or closing-down stage. It is very much in the spirit of creative problem-solving for the decision to draw on the intuitions of those involved in the enactment of the decisions. This might be seen as the creative discovery or Eureka moment, very much a right-brain process. Or it might involve a more analytical approach. Creativity researchers have retained interest in the creativity diamond, and in finding refinements in ways of opening up options and in making effective decisions.

After Osborn's early work on brainstorming, creativity techniques began to incorporate more creativity diamonds. At each stage of the three diamonds in the MPIA approach, techniques for opening up and closing down are applied. (We will suggest later that the idea and action diamonds can be compressed into one action-idea diamond.)

Dream team diamond   Standard team diamond   Team from hell diamond

Figure 3.7 Search patterns of a dream team, a standard team and a team from hell

Dream teams, with or without deliberate application of techniques, search each diamond widely, and develop a wider range of options from which to choose wisely. Other teams need help to widen their search processes.

Figure 3.7 shows the different kinds of search that might be associated with a dream team, standard team and team from hell. The dream team will search in a way that sparks off lateral and unexpected possibilities, at perspectives and idea stages. The standard team stays closely to the preconceived thoughts, perspectives and ideas of the team members. The team from hell may have an even narrower range of search than that achieved by the members working in isolation.

In the next three chapters we will show how creative searches can be widened and how subsequent decisions may be made more effective.

A SIMPLE SITUATION EXPLORED USING MPIA VOCABULARY

MPIA thinking helps us to new insights into our behaviours, and how these behaviours are supporting or blocking new ideas. We can appreciate the approach by applying it to a simple situation – a very short play in three acts.

> Act One. An apartment building, very early in the morning. The door opens and a man steps out. He shuts the door firmly and walks towards his parked car. Before reaching the car he stops and fumbles in his pocket for his keys. He does not find his keys.

> Act Two. The man returns to the apartment building and tries the handle of the door. The door remains locked. He then repeats the process of searching for his keys, beginning in his trouser pockets. He then walks to the car and tries the doors of the car. He cannot open the car doors.

> Act Three. He returns to the front door of the apartment, still fumbling in his pockets for his keys. As he is nearing the door he shakes his head, pauses, and then sets off purposively past his car towards the corner of the street where he disappears from our view.

According to the MPIA model we might say he is acting as if the problem is finding his keys. That is his dominant perspective. His main idea is that his keys 'should be' in his pockets. The more often he repeats the search in his pockets, the more he is in a 'stuckness' loop. At some point he shifts to a different behaviour, suggesting that he has a new perspective. Perhaps he has decided that his priority is not to find his keys, but to get to work on time. Maybe he has changed his plan, and instead of driving to work in his car, he will take a cab. After an uncertain start he is able to make a break with his dominant mind-set and follow a new approach.

This simple solution can be used as a metaphor for all kinds of individual and team behaviours. When a team hits difficulties it is at first inclined to test out the situation in terms of mind-sets. Gradually a dominant belief or perspective emerges. We see the mapping process as exposing the main components of basic beliefs and assumptions. If the team agrees to the nature of the change it is moving to the perspective stage. Under typical conditions, suggestions or ideas follow team agreement about the nature of the problem. These are dominated by the shared beliefs or platform of understanding. Ideas stay close to old ideas. Actions stay close to old actions.

Creativity supporting techniques seek to generate more powerful ideas. The MPIA works at the process of getting behind the assumptions of the mind-map to reveal new perspectives and from these to discover new and valuable action-ideas.

MORE ABOUT THE MPIA STRUCTURE

The MPIA system is designed to enable a team working with a complex issue to move from thinking to reaching starting-points for action. It is based on many years' experience of working with such issues in a diversity of circumstances and in many different cultures. As we have suggested, it is not an ideas sausage machine, where you put a complicated issue in at one end and a perfect idea pops out at the other. Rather it is designed to help you understand the scope of a project, find some starting perspectives and use them to generate novel, actionable ideas to help the team to make progress. No doubt you will be relieved to learn that it is not necessary to apply this structure to every problem you come across in your working life. Where it will help you enormously is in situations in which you are required to take action where at least some of the aspects are not clear.

Each application calls for a contribution from the team, and particularly from the creative leader, in fine-tuning the MPIA to circumstances. Some of the variations will be covered in the following chapters. These can be

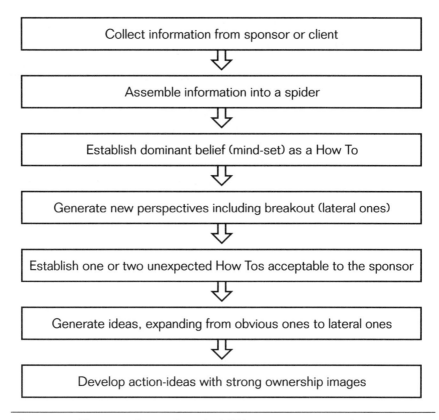

Figure 3.8   The general procedures for MPIA in creative teamwork

accommodated within a basic version indicated in Figure 3.8. Readers unacquainted with creativity techniques are advised to spend some time becoming familiar with these stages before proceeding any further.

MESSES AND MAPS

For some years we imagined the first stage of the creative process as a struggle with a messy situation. M stood for mess. More recently we have felt that, if there is conscious effort at examining the mess, the activity might be better described as mapping. A mess is more appropriate for the early work before there has been any effort at structuring the information. Rather than add another M-stage to the MPIA we see a mess as a very indistinct map.

The conscious use of MPIA means that the early efforts are directed towards mapping as a way of making the information easier to understand. In our practical work we have not found any difficulties in using mapping to describe deliberate efforts, and mess to indicate the less structured early stages of creative work.

All complex situations have many facets to them and it is important that these are noted as quickly as possible, ideally at the very beginning of the project. For this we recommend the use of a spider diagram, described in more detail in Chapter 4. Our old friend mind-set plays a huge part in influencing which part of any project brief team members will think important. At the mapping stage, the person drawing the spider should make notes of all suggestions. If they are not relevant, they will drop out later. Arguing at this stage can waste a great deal of time. However you make your map, find a way of preserving it. This is the start of your platform of understanding and you will save a great deal of time if you keep it as a frame of reference.

PERSPECTIVES

Once you have your map to guide you, you are ready to move to the next stage of the structure, the perspectives stage which is covered in detail in Chapter 5. Here we want to explain briefly why the perspective stage is so important.

A multi-faceted situation has many starting-points for action. In most routine situations they are relatively limited and we can move on without too much agonizing; this is what makes them routine. Complex, open-ended situations require a different approach. The perspectives in a situation (phrased in our structure as 'How To' statements) reflect the differing experiences and concerns within a team and are used to provide a focus for idea generation. In any moderately complex situation you might expect between 15 and 20 How To statements.

There is a temptation once the mapping stage has been completed to pick one topic and plunge straight into generating ideas. The How To stage is designed to hold you back from that, to make sure that you have considered several possibilities at the outset.

IDEA GENERATION

At last, you say, we arrive at the really creative stage. However, we would prefer to regard what you have been doing in the earlier stages as creative as well. Remember that creativity is the development of what is new and valuable. You will already have been creative in discovering the clusters of patterns of information at the mapping stage. Powerful new perspectives are also a result of creative insights.

DISTINGUISHING PERSPECTIVES FROM IDEAS

When introduced to the MPIA system, many people at first find it difficult to appreciate the difference between an idea and a perspective or How To statement. This is partly because, in everyday speech, the term idea is used to mean any kind of thought. Ideas might refer to daydreams, to plans, or to solutions to problems.

Within the MPIA system we differentiate between these various outputs of mental activity. A perspective is a special kind of thought that indicates a desired goal or objective. To remind us of its special status we tag it with the prefix 'How To'. We need a vocabulary of this kind to challenge preconceived beliefs. A team that discovers a new How To is well on the way to breaking out of its old assumptions. The prevailing goal may be accidentally restricting its scope for action, for example.

A How To will provide a starting-point for a different kind of mental output, namely ideas. This is often where confusion begins, because some ideas seem rather close to new perspectives. Indeed, they can be turned into new perspectives simply by applying the How To prefix. Such ideas generally do not imply a clear visualizable action. It follows that the confusion can be overcome as a team acquires the creative habit of building more actions into their ideas.

In Part II we devote a whole chapter to ways of generating powerful How Tos. We also devote a chapter to ways of making ideas more action-oriented.

In the MPIA system, ideas are generated around a few selected perspectives. A key issue in effective idea generation is focus. Brainstorming for ideas is like running a 100-metre sprint. Your How To is the signal to settle in the starting blocks. When the gun sounds, go! You did not see great sprinters like Linford Christie or Carl Lewis leave the blocks and then stop or slow down halfway through the race, wondering what they should be doing. They have carried out extensive mental preparation beforehand to enable them to concentrate solely on reaching that line; they had their platform of understanding. Within the MPIA structure, about 30 minutes of good-quality idea generation, using idea-spurring techniques, should be adequate.

When the MPIA system is applied after training, participants will be using the lateral thinking techniques and the Yes And approach at this stage. These methods keep the ideas flowing, and the Yes And serves as the most simple and direct means of developing a positive climate.

ACTIONS

We have separated the ideas and action stages, so that we can emphasize the importance of working on promising ideas. In reality, these two stages are intertwined and often difficult to separate. The important point at the action stage is to understand that the team is advised to concentrate on idea ownership, in order to make the ideas more action-oriented.

Action-ideas flow from more visual contributions to team work. As already discussed, visualization has become an important aspect of creative problem-solving. This might be said to require whole-brain contributions, within which efforts are directed towards creating a mental picture in which team members develop 'owned' actions for themselves.

Summary

This chapter began with the story of a successful team admitting that they had nearly left it too late to apply structured creativity. For any complex situation demanding novel outcomes, the advice is be creative from the outset! In this context creativity is defined as novelty plus added value. Novelty by itself is not enough; to be creative in the work context you need ideas that are actionable and relevant to the situation.

We make sense of the world around us through mental filters. Termed mind-sets, these filters derive from our experience, education, expertise and expectations and can make us over-sensitive to some types of information and blind to others. When circumstances change mind-sets persist, perhaps leading to 'stuckness'. Creative problem-solving techniques help us to become more aware of our mind-sets and give us tools to help us challenge them. They also help us to integrate left- and right-brain thinking approaches to problem-solving and to deal with complicated open-ended situations more effectively.

Unless we find creative escapes, team performance is likely to remain at a standard level of competence. We looked at the metaphoric and lateral options for boosting creativity, then examined the MPIA model.

The key to the successful use of the MPIA approach is to regard it as a system to guide creative learning. Practice makes it possible for a team to recognize potential blocking situations and learn to deal with them effectively. As teams gain experience they will be able to improve their standard of performance and aspire to dream team status.

PART *II*

CREATIVE TEAMS IN PRACTICE

Each of the three chapters in Part II explores a particular aspect of the MPIA system. Readers can work their way through the chapters as a means of becoming acquainted with the MPIA system for enhancing team creativity. This is always best if it is combined with practical teamwork, which in turn provides learning opportunities. If, alternatively, readers are part of a team that has already trained in an approach for enhancing its performance they will be able to use the chapters to strengthen operation of their existing system.

One of the secrets of dream teams is learning from experience. Our own preference would be for teams to allow for review periods, especially as the decision to set aside time is itself a commitment towards team development. Don't be put off by shortage of time. Find some. The team that has no time for review has no time for changing its practices. (And if you always do what you've always done, you'll always get what you've always got.)

A structure for review might be as follows. Find a focus – for example, the application of a particular set of techniques such as the mapping systems described in Chapter 4. Examine a specific experience. Then compare the mapping process outlined with previous behaviours. If you did no formal mapping, what activities were serving to build a platform of understanding? Are there ways in which the seven secrets of dream teams are strengthened by the new structures? What procedures might be done differently in a specified future activity?

Repeat the review process for finding new perspectives covered in Chapter 5 and again for creating action-ideas described in Chapter 6.

4 FROM MESSES TO MIND-MAPS

A spider to the rescue

One bright summer morning a cargo plane on a routine flight from Amsterdam to Manchester hit the runway hard. The cargo shifted and the plane went nose-up. Like all well-drilled teams, the airport's emergency services were quickly into action. Such incidents are statistically rare and simulations are the means whereby the teams are able to act in emergencies as if they had to be dealt with every week.

The comprehensive manual of instructions can never anticipate every specific detail of an incident. That is why human initiative is still required. By a coincidence the duty officer had attended a creative team meeting just days before and one technique had stuck in his mind: 'To get the facts down quickly, use a spider diagram.' As the team members assembled he had time to note down the specific feature of this incident. Within minutes he and his colleagues had begun the sequence of events that were to ensure effective communication and to minimize risks to all personnel concerned.

The incident was dealt with in the customary professional fashion. The duty officer later confessed that his swiftly directed instructions had benefited from the few minutes he had devoted to drawing up a spider diagram. 'They think I showed a great deal of skill,' he commented. 'That's what I'm trained to do. But there was also a lot of team work between us, helped by a spider diagram.'

Overview

In this chapter we shall look at the rationale of mind-mapping. Our own work owes much to the pioneering efforts of Tony Buzan who has drawn attention to the potential of mind-maps, often associated with his name as Buzan Diagrams. The techniques covered here are those that deal with the knowledge that a team brings to bear in a given situation. The process is an excellent one for building a platform of understanding. As team members make contributions, the information provides clues about those aspects that are shared, and those that are more individualistic, perhaps open to discussion or dispute. We like to talk of a platform of understanding that can be strengthened by openness but perhaps undermined by less collaborative group behaviours.

The general principle behind mind-mapping

Mind-mapping can occur in a mind-boggling number of ways, only some of which we have indicated. Furthermore, mind-mappers will apply available resources in different ways. The simplest approach to understanding these activities is through consideration of the general principles behind them.

The activities of mind-mapping involve participation and information-sharing, without immediate evaluation or rejection of diverse or even contradictory suggestions. The principle is that of sensitizing through direct experience. The specific or surface activities are necessary but can have a multitude of forms. The general principle is that learning follows a 'surfacing' of beliefs that are often hidden from consciousness. Once sensitized to the 'already present' beliefs, someone can do something about them – perhaps by challenging the revealed mapping to consider other ways of making sense of things.

But why do we put such emphasis on direct experience? Because commitment is gained as a team constructs its mind-map together as a direct and fresh experience. The similarities that are acknowledged build trust. The differences that surface are important as trigger-points for new thinking and team discoveries.

FROM MESSES TO MAPS

The team brought together for a shared task never begins with a straightforward picture of what is needed. This was recognized by Operations Research specialists attempting to bring formalization and scientific principles into dealing with complex problems. They popularized the expression 'mess' to indicate a team's starting situation and its prevailing uncertainties. One particularly difficult issue is where to draw the boundaries of a messy problem. Implicit in the work was the belief that scientific analysis could help the team out of the mess and that the result would be a clarification of the 'real' problem.

There is much to be said for the vocabulary of messiness in complex problem-solving. For some years we taught that the preliminary stage in creative problem-solving was dealing with the mess. Where creative problem-solving differs from these analytical systems, however, is in its rejection of the objective status of a 'real problem' identifiable in isolation from the problem-owners. To indicate the difference in emphasis we have recently chosen to label the first stage in the MPIA a 'mapping' stage.

The remainder of the chapter will cover a few important aspects of managing the mapping process. We then deal in some detail with an all-purpose mapping approach – spider diagrams – before touching on other ways of constructing maps within creative teamwork.

Notes on mapping

WHY IS MAPPING IMPORTANT?

In the history of innovations, the role of the map is severely underestimated. Early explorers drew their own maps as much for themselves as for those who came after them. An adventurer needed a map to return to the place where provisions had been stored, or even where treasure had been buried. A map is generally a powerful source of information, of particular value in journeys of exploration.

TWO SORTS OF MAPS

When teams examine their situation and plan ahead, they are engaging in a kind of map-making. The process is the rather special one in which the map is made for the people who intend to use it. The map-makers and map-readers are the same people. We can call these maps customized for the purposes of the users. The more common kind of map is supplied ready-made and cannot easily be customized.

Customized maps	Supplied maps
Map-users are map-makers	Map-users are not map-makers
Map-making creates platform of understanding	Map-making clarifies platform of understanding
Users impose unique meanings on the map	Map imposes its meaning on users

Figure 4.1   Customized and supplied maps

The map-making captures the team's platform of understanding. This means that a team from hell is unable to make much of a map. Its failure to do so is one more indication of its inadequacies in any activity calling for collaboration. Standard teams build standard maps containing well-known features. As shown in Figure 4.1, standard teams might just as well be given a pre-made map. Dream teams create maps, the process in itself also serving to strengthen the shared understanding among the map-builders.

WHOSE MAP IS IT ANYWAY?

There is an important point to be recognized about the map-making stage of the MPIA process. The mapping is intended to support the platform of understanding of the team working to a specific purpose. The MPIA aims to produce new actions. The owner or owners of the map are those people whose actions will change as a consequence of the creative activities of the team.

In drawing up a map, it is a good starting point to ask 'Whose map is it?' as in Figure 4.2. One type of map may be drawn up as a way of strengthening

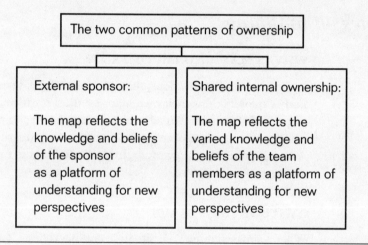

Figure 4.2   Whose map is it anyway?

the platform of understanding with a sponsor or client who is not a core member of the team. Such a map should be treated as temporary. When presenting it to its sponsor, the team is asking for confirmation that it represents the salient features of the sponsor's situation. Under these circumstances, the team should resist the temptation of mapping a world through the eyes of its members. The representation is of what the sponsor sees as reality.

The second profile is one in which the team has more control over the map. In effect the team becomes its own sponsor. Then the construction of the map is far more interactive. The process of building a platform of understanding still persists, however.

THE CARTOGRAPHER'S ROLE

Map-building is a creative activity. We are not just talking about the actual drawing of the map. The encouragement of the team members and the development of a creative climate both require creative leadership. Here, as in other parts of the MPIA process, the requirements can be divided into task leadership skills (drawing up the map) and process leadership skills for team development (drawing out the group).

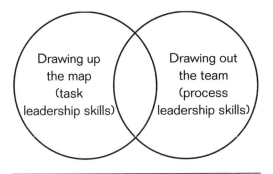

The two roles overlap as shown in Figure 4.3. Some teams find it more acceptable and effective to have two different people conducting the roles at any given time. Other teams prefer one leader to do both, although this is particularly challenging. In these circumstances it becomes particularly important for the mapper/leader to make it clear at the start that every one in the team has to participate supportively to make the mapping a success.

Figure 4.3 The overlapping skills of map-building

As illustrated in Figure 4.4, the mapper's golden rule is that each contribution from a team member has to be recorded: 'If it's worth thinking it's worth saying . . . If it's worth saying, its worth writing down.'

The leader role, whether combined with that of map-maker or not, is to encourage the constructive and open behaviours associated with a creative

Figure 4.4 The first principle of map-building

climate as discussed in Chapter 2. The process leader's golden rule is to invite support as often and as widely as possible from team members. There is a strong case for rotating the roles to some degree. This helps to sustain a team climate in which there is flexibility and acceptance of shared responsibilities. It helps to develop useful skills among the team members.

We have completed our notes on the mapping process in general. We will now review some of the most common mapping techniques, beginning with our favourite, the spider diagram.

Spider diagrams

Our preferred approach for mapping activities is based on the team constructing a mind-map or spider diagram. The technique is particularly suitable because it is one of the simplest. It requires very little in the way of resources, it is acceptable to a wide range of users and a wide range of situations, and it can be quickly understood and applied. That is why we have advocated its use to many teams and why we give it high priority here.

TO PRODUCE A SPIDER DIAGRAM

1 Turn the paper sideways (you can make more use of the space).
2 Start writing in the centre of the page, with the topic in the body of the spider.
3 Put descriptions of between six and eight key themes – one for each 'leg' of the spider.
4 Build sub-themes ('fingers and toes').
5 Look for links and connections between the themes.
6 Enhance the diagram by using different colours for different kinds of themes.
7 Redraw if needed after reviewing – you may have a quite different view of things then.

REDRAWING THE SPIDER

In a team which is following the MPIA process for creative work, the spider diagram makes the platform of understanding more visible in the context of a specific task or problem. Drawing the spider encourages dialogue about this platform of understanding. Discussion of improved versions of the spider continues this process of learning. The study of the spider, with or without redrawing, is a good way to prepare the group for moving attention towards the P and IA activities that are to follow.

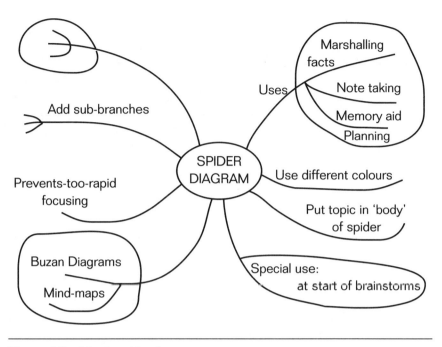

Figure 4.5   A basic spider diagram

ADMISSIBLE EVIDENCE

Strongly influenced by mind-sets from training and education, business teams have a preference for sticking to facts. Feelings tend to be suppressed as inadmissible evidence to the court in many work contexts. Unsubstantiated facts and rumours are also discouraged. The creative team should be more open to sharing its feelings and concerns. On the basis that 'If it's worth thinking it's worth saying, and writing down' there is a place for any of these kinds of offerings on the spider. Most teamwork involves emotions. If the norms of behaviour suppress them, the outcome is likely to be weak on the human aspects of the work.

DEALING WITH MUTANT SPIDERS

When left without instructions, teams tend to assemble spiders in ways that reveal a weak platform of understanding. Two common forms of 'mutant spider' are shown in Figure 4.6.

The first is one in which the team struggles to find more than two or three important aspects of the task being considered. This will become a source of

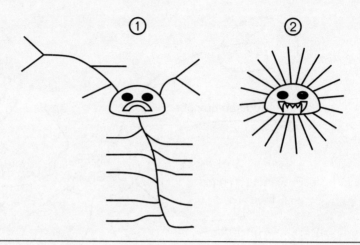

Figure 4.6 Beware mutant spiders!

weakness as the team tries to break out of particularly powerful mind-sets. A team that produces a mutant spider may need further assistance in mind-mapping, perhaps on a warm-up task that its members find less difficult to work with. More positively, the process has potentially given the team a powerful hint as to the bias in their thinking. Under some initial guidance, the team can apply itself to build a more powerful platform of understanding.

The second common pattern is a drawing that more closely resembles a centipede than a spider. The drawing is all legs and no secondary 'fingers and toes'. The team may express a number of ideas, but it has not been able to agree what might be the most important themes under consideration. A team that produces such a centipede may be advised to redraw it into a spider, perhaps after a break to discuss the most important aspects. Once again, the distorted outcome of one set of actions can become a focus for improvement.

OTHER TECHNICAL AND TECHNICOLOUR HINTS

For breakout groups of two to four people, the spider can be drawn by a nominated map-maker in the team as discussion continues. A few minutes are often adequate for map-making in such cases.

An exclusion principle in this, or any other kind of map-making, is that the 'map-owner' is better occupied concentrating on sharing his or her knowledge with the other team members. Someone else should look after the mapping and process leadership duties.

DEMONSTRATING THE CREATIVE ASPECT OF THE MAPPING PROCESS

It is easy to demonstrate the creative aspect of mapping to team members who have not experienced the process before, particularly using spider diagrams. The exercise begins with the experienced facilitator describing the process. Then the team members are asked to work individually on a topic likely to involve them. In setting up this exercise it is advisable to refrain from mentioning what the topic is until after the participants have had the process explained to them. Once the topic is mentioned, the participants tend to become focused on the task and less able to listen to instructions about the method. The invitation might be framed in the following terms.

I want each team member to build a personal spider diagram. Work outwards from the body of the spider in the middle of a blank sheet of paper. Each time you think of some important aspect of the topic, draw a leg coming off from the body of the spider and label it with the main idea. You will find that each leg triggers off other ideas that fit on to it (fingers and toes if you like!). Five to ten minutes should be enough for you to appreciate the way the technique works and for you to construct the main 'shape' of the information. Whatever comes to mind, try to write it down, and find a place for it on the spider. The topic for the centre of the spider is . . .

Some thought should be given to suggesting a topic that appeals to the interests of team members, perhaps evoking memories of a personal kind. Successful topics have included the following, with the italicized phrase or word appropriate for the centre of the spider.

- My next family *holiday*
- How *my department* works (you have been asked unexpectedly to talk to a visiting trade delegation)
- *Moving house*
- A *retirement speech* for a colleague
- Improving my *promotion* prospects
- My favourite *hobby* (after-dinner speech)

A good time for a break is after the team has completed their first spider. At this point, team members and especially the map-owners can be encouraged to revisit the spider. The process of reflection may lead to further and deeper discussion and any new points should be quickly added to the spider before the team moves to the next stage.

The spider can be made more engaging in various ways. Coloured felt-tip pens are of considerable value both for brightening up the picture and for distinguishing different kinds of information. More artistic contributions to the spider can also be well received. However, the individual who treats the process as an opportunity for artistic therapy may eventually test the patience of other team members.

WHAT CAPTION GOES IN THE MIDDLE OF THE SPIDER?

Inexperienced groups argue about the caption for the middle of the spider. This amounts to the title of a drawing that is about to be constructed.

Some groups see it as the 'what' or the simplest short description available. The caption describes the topic under discussion. The 'what' permits subsequent development of the who, when and where issues that tend to be found on the legs of the spider.

The 'what' helps the team draw a crude boundary around the topic for discussion although there may still be disagreements about making the topic more or less complex. Two factors should be emphasized in this respect. First, the caption can always be treated as provisional. If the spider construction suggests that changing the caption would be helpful, that is always possible, but best done after a decent attempt has been made to construct the spider

using the initial suggestion. Second, the caption is one small contribution to building a platform of understanding. If agreement is a long time in coming, it may be important to take a break and explore what might be the misunderstandings inhibiting the task development. In other words, when there are problems with the task, check the group dynamics.

Other mapping procedures

POST-IT® NOTES

Trainers and consultants have been ingenious in finding applications for these famous little pads of low-stick paper. Arguably the only restriction to their use is the need for a large surface to assemble them into a mind-map.

Almost certainly any new user will find their own way of using them within the general principle of mind-mapping. Our example comes from the technical development department of a multinational manufacturer of computer systems that has achieved the highest awards for its quality standards. Within each team project, the team leaders follow a highly documented approach for developing improvements to eliminate defects and to raise performance standards. Additionally they have free-ranging sessions for identifying areas for targeting future projects.

We had demonstrated 'our' spider diagram approach to mapping and had been invited to see their alternative approach. We watched a team that had found a space to conduct a quick meeting within the large conference room on site. They worked standing up, around a very large and expensive white back-projection screen for computer graphics. However, on this occasion the team was in a very low-tech operating mode. The leader (who was a trained facilitator) issued a pad of Post-it notes to each team member. In a few minutes each member had written his or her priority areas for future projects, one for each Post-it note. Then the team gathered even closer around the whiteboard and began to build up the mind-map from its Post-it components. Clusters of themes emerged, with some elements being moved around with a great deal of enthusiasm and humour as participants explained their rationale. Disputed 'places' eventually led to the reconstruction of parts of the map and its clusters. The trainer explained that the process usually generated about six or seven clusters with up to 20 elements in each.

We subsequently discussed the relative merits of spiders and Post-its as mapping techniques with those team members who had experienced both. The general consensus was probably a willingness to work with either system, but an intention to use the more familiar one unless pressed to do otherwise.

HEXAGONS

The hexagon system is a training and consulting innovation that we have come across in use in several UK organizations. Each hexagon has an adhesive back surface (magnetic versions are common) and a front surface with wipe-clean properties, thus offering an advantage over Post-its. The sets of hexagons can be assembled and reassembled on any convenient surfaces.

One group of internal consultants in a large public sector division are often invited to support planning meetings, with the request 'Come and bring those hexagons with you.' This group became acquainted with spider diagrams after some experience of hexagons. Typically they favour hexagons in a small planning meeting, only preferring spider diagrams if the hexagons are in use by another facilitator or if the request involves larger numbers of teams (not enough hexagons to go around).

CARDS AND BROWN PAPER

Our experiences of the cards and brown-paper mapping methods have been mostly as observers rather than participants. One well-tried system is Metaplan, a structured approach to information mapping and idea generation. Developed by a German architect to encourage large group consultation concerning building plans, it involves mapping information on cards and using these to cluster information and generate problem formulations. Idea generation is by interactive and nominal group brainstorming. During the idea generation phase, courteous behaviour is encouraged by the suggestion that 'You should be your neighbour's butler.' This has particular value in dealing with complex problems that require the commitment of a large group of people. As with all such systems, training is needed to use the system to maximum effect.

The specialized uses of the system have been applied within extremely thorough systems analysis, for example, within Business Process Re-engineering efforts in the mid-1990s. Spider diagrams have structural aspects that encourage teams to find a few key 'legs' or themes. By contrast, in these cases the sheer quantity of information assembled – sometimes literally along the length of an extensive corridor – can produce a sense of information overload. It can also lead to rather unimaginative efforts at dismantling the existing 'platform of understanding' – the general intention behind the exercise.

That is not to suggest that the approach has no merits. Using the Yes And technique we would prefer to state that these more complex systems are needed for fine-detail examination of complex systems. In addition, they may well be augmented by a less detailed kind of mind-mapping to prepare the group for discovering more break-out concepts.

RICH PICTURES

We are sometimes asked why the MPIA approach is so dependent on written words. Why is there a preference for the verbal in our system whereas creativity is often connected with non-verbal images and concepts? Our view is that the platform of understanding is best approached from the communication mode familiar to most teams, that of the written and spoken word. Others, such as design teams, may have different non-verbal modes. It should be added that we encourage non-verbal modes in escaping from abstracted and verbal ones and often incorporate non-verbal images within the spider diagrams. However, there is plenty of scope for creative analysis here for teams who would like to find ways of escaping from the 'tyranny of words' even at the mapping stage.

One well-known graphic, rather than a linguistic, approach to mapping business systems has been developed by Professor Peter Checkland and his colleagues at the University of Lancaster. Their general method, termed soft-systems methodology (SSM), has been extensively tested in analysing complex business systems. It is outside the scope of this book to describe the workings of SSM. Here we are only concerned with its rather unusual visual procedure known as rich picture development. In our schema, this clearly represents an alternative set of M activities to our spider diagrams.

A typical context for its use would be to promote deeper self-awareness of the multiple aspects of a complicated business system through creating a rich picture. We would compare the intentions here with those of a team assembling a spider diagram. One very important difference is the emphasis on diverging completely from the habitual ways of thinking about business systems – thinking that tends to be highly abstract, with its implicitly accepted professional shorthand (accused of being jargon by outsiders).

Developing skills at creating rich pictures can be a powerful aid for teams. One well-known example in the spirit of Checkland's work comes from a long-term project within a Norwegian aluminium smelting plant. The workers and management, with expert facilitative help, built a rich picture of the plant as it was, and as they would like it to become. The pictures contrasted a neglected garden overrun with weeds with a well-tended garden that everyone would be proud to create and maintain.

The shift is encouraged by representing the interacting components as a picture. Related techniques can be found in the work of art therapists where the drawings are believed to help self-discovery and awareness. As far as possible, words have been replaced by vivid images – doodles, symbols with metaphoric significance, and any of the techniques to be found in a work of visual art. Some trainers see such processes as helping a team (or individual) escape from left-brain verbal thinking, and thereby encouraging right-brain images to surface.

A word of caution: thinking in pictures does not come easily to team members who by inclination or professional conditioning have lost the capacity to do something that came to them fairly easily in their early school art classes. First efforts by 'grown-up' teams may be not much more than concealed abstractions. For example, an engineering group that customarily thinks in terms of quality control measures may draw a picture of the dial of a monitoring instrument with a few matchstick figures dotted around (perhaps with unhappy expressions). This is probably no more than a nudge away from their dominant engineering mind-sets. Practice is needed for the pictures created to go beyond rather automatic and lifeless images. Simply going through the motions in a mechanical fashion will not suffice.

As in much of the work in creativity-seeking, grave damage can result from a too-rapid assumption that 'this doesn't work for us'. The inexperienced team may need time and a few successes with more familiar approaches before feeling comfortable with such unfamiliar ones aimed at strengthening mental imagery.

COMPUTER-BASED SYSTEMS

Computer-based mapping systems for individuals and teams have developed since the early days of personal computers. The rise in networked communication systems is encouraging even more rapid development of computer-aided approaches. Most design teams are already familiar with such systems for stimulating creativity. At the time of writing, virtual reality and multi-media approaches are being successfully tested as means of transforming the way in which individuals and teams can study and create new maps of reality. These are exciting and important new possibilities as members of a team find themselves operating at a large physical distance from one another.

Comparing the mapping approaches

To support creative learning, teams are encouraged to find mapping techniques that suit their own requirements. We currently favour spiders, but we also try to keep in touch with developments and experiences of other techniques. In Figure 4.7 we have assessed a few techniques we work with from time to time. We should add that our ratings are subjective and should not be taken as a 'Which Guide'. Readers have to make up their own matrix, based on their own experiences and judgements.

Summary

The chapter began with the example of an operational manager using a spider diagram to deal with a complicated situation. The subsequent actions taken by the manager illustrate the benefits of carrying out the mapping stage before moving to action mode. The mapping process allows teams to become aware of what they take for granted in a situation, and what may be hidden.

Mapping from the direct experience of the team is important, because commitment is gained as team members construct a mind map together. Differences that surface can act as important trigger points for new thinking and team discoveries.

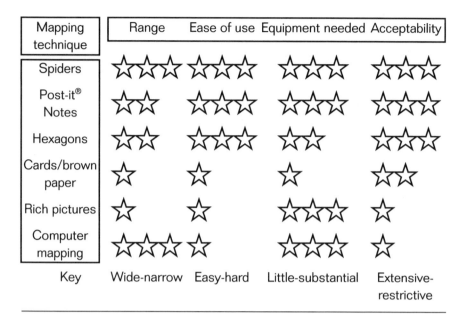

Mapping technique	Range	Ease of use	Equipment needed	Acceptability
Spiders	☆☆☆	☆☆☆	☆☆☆	☆☆☆
Post-it® Notes	☆☆	☆☆☆	☆☆☆	☆☆☆
Hexagons	☆☆	☆☆☆	☆☆	☆☆☆
Cards/brown paper	☆	☆	☆	☆☆
Rich pictures	☆	☆	☆☆☆	☆
Computer mapping	☆☆☆☆	☆	☆☆☆	☆
Key	Wide-narrow	Easy-hard	Little-substantial	Extensive-restrictive

Figure 4.7 Alternative mapping approaches

Map-making helps to build the team's platform of understanding and can act as an indicator to its future performance. A team from hell with a weak platform will be unable to map effectively. Standard teams produce standard maps and, without collective and discovery learning, will rarely break out of mind-sets. Dream teams create their maps together and the creative climate they share adds to their understanding. They produce a customized map that is fit for the requirements they face.

Who owns a map? Those whose actions will change as a consequence of the creative activities of the team. We describe two common profiles of ownership: a team working to an external brief and a team carrying out a task owned within the team. In the first case, the map is used to build an understanding between the team and its project client. In the second case, the process strengthens understanding within the team.

Map-building is a creative activity. As in other parts of the MPIA process, leading the team requires task leadership skills (drawing up the map) and process leadership skills (drawing out the group). Every contribution must be recorded for task and process reasons. The mapper's golden rule is 'If it's worth thinking it's worth saying . . . If it's worth saying, it's worth writing down.'

Our preferred mapping technique, the spider diagram, was described in some detail. We feel it is particularly important that a team becomes aware of what constitutes admissible evidence in their work environment. Neglecting what's normally inadmissible may lead to a mutant spider!

Other mapping approaches are all valuable tools in the mapper's kitbag. We have found excellent practical applications for Post-it notes, hexagons, brown paper wall charts and rich picture systems. Computer-based systems have the advantage that the maps are easy to store and can be readily retrieved at future sessions.

5 BREAKTHROUGH PERSPECTIVES

Breakthrough thinking on the oil rigs

In February 1998, the Shell Exploration group announced that one of its production teams had found ways of increasing oil production figures from North Sea rigs by one per cent. In an industry where fractions of a per cent can mean millions of dollars in revenue, any 'easy' improvements in productivity have been implemented many years ago. The achievement was therefore a tribute to teamwork of the highest order. We were reminded of some earlier work with such a dream team within the petroleum exploration and production business.

At the time, the team was aware of the potential benefits from upgrading the control systems on the oil rigs. The logistics of such maintenance work on the rigs are notoriously tricky. Shuttling a team of information technologists backwards and forwards was likely to prove both expensive and reliant on unpredictable weather conditions. Jeremy, an enthusiast for the MPIA creative thinking approach, supported the project team. With his encouragement, the team carried out a conventional analysis and then began to consider more unusual possibilities.

'There's no way we can shift these characters backwards and forwards on budget. There's no real way of knowing what it's going to cost. Except we know it'll cost plenty.'

'Wouldn't it be wonderful if we could guarantee fine weather?' Jeremy suggested.

The team looked at Jeremy as if he had gone mad. Fine weather guaranteed in the North Sea? 'It's bad enough here on land,' someone commented. 'And we aren't doing the refit here.'

'Well, why not do the refit here?'

The team became interested at that. After the inevitable Yes Buts, they agreed there might just be a way. Jeremy went on to visit other teams for which he was offering a creative support service. A few weeks later he received a telephone call from the team leader. 'You might like to come up to see what we've set up,' suggested the leader, refusing to explain further. When Jeremy returned the team took him to a workshop where he found, to his astonishment, a full-scale model of the control panels of an oil rig. At first he could not work out how they had done it at such speed and (as they admitted) on a tight budget.

'Once we rethought the problem we had something new to aim for,' the team leader explained. 'We had been moving designers, IT specialists and operators out to the rigs. But we knew the full details of the control panels. The problem was the cost of moving people around. So we wondered how to build a simulated control system cheaply. Angus knew exactly how we could do that. He's in the local amateur dramatic society and they build all their own sets. They were happy with what we could pay them for building us a mock-up. Then we did the redesign and training work here. Not bad, eh?' Jeremy agreed.

Perspectives thinking

Jeremy is a highly regarded information technologist who is also a skilled team facilitator. The example indicates some of his efforts at directing the team's attention towards new perspectives – the How Tos of the MPIA model. The How To approach is the subject of this chapter. We will never know whether the team would have arrived at their particular breakthough without Jeremy's intervention. That is the nature of real-life examples. But we would agree with the view expressed by the team that his approach probably made all the difference.

Just as we have a favourite or 'default' technique at the mapping stage (spider diagrams), we have a favourite technique to encourage teams to think creatively at the perspective stage. This is the How To . . .
approach.

So strong is our belief in How Tos that we are prepared to go to considerable lengths to reinforce their potential for change among would-be team members. When working with such teams, one of us has been known to interrupt overheard conversations at coffee breaks if there has been no evidence of a wide search for new perspectives. The cry of 'Don't forget your How Tos' is mostly taken in good humour and sometimes provides a 'jolt' leading to new perspectives.

Overview

In this chapter we look at the dynamics of a team following the MPIA approach, focusing on the P for perspectives. We see how standard teams generate standard perspectives that are closely linked with the teams' standard map or information base (platform of understanding). In the MPIA system, the standard team may stick closely to the How Tos implied in their spider diagram. To break through the glass ceiling of standard performance calls for creative approaches at the P-stage. The creative process can be improved if the leadership style encourages 'flow and stretch' – a form of brainstorming at the stage of perspective-seeking.

The new perspectives have been produced in a climate that encourages openness to new possibilities. That is why idea ownership processes begin here. Discovery will always involve uncertainties. Through this process, a greater support is offered for the intuitive selection of promising How Tos by subsequent idea owners.

The power of perspectives

FROM PROBLEMS TO PERSPECTIVES

The P-stage of MPIA refers to the perspective-seeking and choosing stage. We feel that the term perspective has several advantages over problems, a term we used previously. We switched to perspective because we found users were prone to stay in an earlier mind-set associated with problems. Many people consider a problem to have a logical answer or solution or as having objective and fixed boundaries. This leaves them very much in either-or territory. We wanted a way of helping people to break out from either-or thinking.

Another important distinction is that problems are often treated as abstract entities that do not belong to anyone. Team members who take an 'objective' view distance their descriptions of problems from problem-owners. In contrast, perspectives are, above all, 'owned'. Perspectives thinking also acknowledges a powerful sense of multiple perspectives – 'My way is my way not the way.' This is very much in accord with the mutuality principle. It leads to ways of creating a shared view that 'our way is both my way and your way' as in Figure 5.1.

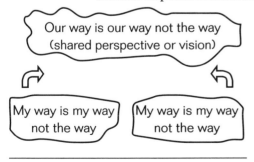

Figure 5.1 The mutuality principle and perspectives

One participant who had been puzzling over the difference commented, 'I suppose you could say that a perspective is a problem with attitude.' We agree. It spells out a very different approach to change. Unless otherwise indicated, someone talking about a problem is likely to be assuming there is a solution.

PERSPECTIVE-SEEKING IS A CREATIVE PROCESS

The opening up of our thought processes to new perspectives is where creative thinking starts to pay off. Professor Csikszentmihalyi at the University of Chicago has been studying the processes of creativity over a period of many years. His conclusion is that creativity emerges as individuals discover a new understanding about the essential aspects of their daily tasks and challenges. He has argued that the process is that of discovery or problem-finding. This is not the same as wandering around looking for trouble. Rather, it is the process by which we become sensitized to liberating ways of thinking. Put another way, the repeated failure to solve a problem may be due to a problem-orientation or understanding that only leads to poor ideas for its resolution. Creative insights are those discoveries that reshape our sense of what we should be doing.

Many examples abound in business of the switch made in answer to the question 'What business are we (now) in?' It was common for business people to answer 'We are in the business of making these high-class widgets . . .' Facing declining sales and profits, other perspectives were found and a whole movement had sprung up from an appreciation of the value of the perspective 'We are in the business of meeting the needs of customers.'

More recently a well-known manufacturer of DIY electric drills announced a breakthrough. Instead of thinking about their business as selling drills, they began to see it as selling holes of required sizes. Such a fresh perspective suggested many new ideas.

Deriving How Tos from the mapping of spiders

The How To approach is one that brings the goals of the team to the surface and sometimes, in addition, the goals of others networked with the team. We can see the mapping process as outlining the terrain, and the How To process as sorting out plans for moving through it. It follows that the caption in the middle of a spider avoids the How To vocabulary.

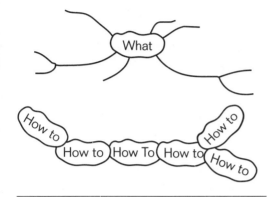

Figure 5.2 How perspectives flow from the mapping process

THE LIMITS OF MECHANISTIC GENERATION OF PERSPECTIVES

Some teams examine the spider diagram and find simple one-to-one relationships between pieces of information on the spider and possible perspectives for the team to consider, as shown in Figure 5.3. Without creative leadership, this process will only confirm the team in its previous understanding of the situation. The body of the spider suggests the most dominant How To. The main overlapping secondary How Tos are suggested by the legs of the spider. The fingers and toes of the spider suggest minor How Tos.

The consequence of such an examination is an agreement that the team 'knows where it stands'. It is also a signal of a team still coming to terms with the potential of the MPIA system to encourage breakthrough thinking. At this stage the performance is that of a standard team (teams from hell find various and unsatisfactory ways of completing the spider, failing to convert even the limited information of their spider into How Tos).

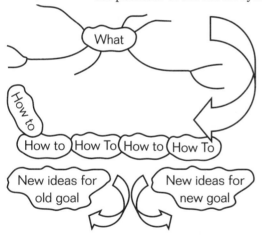

Figure 5.3 Lateral leaps produce new ideas for old or new goals

With leadership help, the process can be made more creative. Examining the data on the spider opens up the team to new possibilities. Old perspectives become clearer, but so do new possibilities. The newly appreciated How To (as in the case of the control panel team) suggests new ideas for existing goals, or may even show why a new goal offers promise and new ideas as in Figure 5.3.

Improving perspective seeking: flowing and stretching

In Chapter 3 we suggested that the search processes of dream teams were wider than those of standard teams. It is easy to see that a standard approach to a spider diagram would produce roughly the same standard output as is strongly dictated by the information on the legs of the spider.

In his book *Creative Problem-Solving*, Sidney Parnes recalls the general approach developed by Alex Osborn and himself. Together with many associates they worked on ways of improving Osborn's original brainstorming method, at first concentrating on ways of enriching idea generation. They found two overlapping methods: ways of enhancing the 'flow' of ideas and ways of enhancing the development 'stretch' or unexpected ideas. Later they realized that the methods could be applied effectively to other stages within their problem-solving approach.

Within the MPIA model, we have developed ways for encouraging teams to flow and stretch. The general approaches are similar for both perspective-seeking and idea-seeking. The context will always have some similarities to a brainstorming session, although the leader may well not make any direct references to brainstorming. Figure 5.4 indicates the two mutually reinforcing sets of interventions available in a session directed by an experienced process leader – flowing and stretching – which we consider now in turn.

ENCOURAGING A FLOW OF PERSPECTIVES

Setting a creative climate can only partly be achieved within a creativity session. A whole gamut of team-building and training approaches is possible and available. Without attention to longer-term team development, however, the one-off session is unlikely to be very successful. Indeed, the chances of

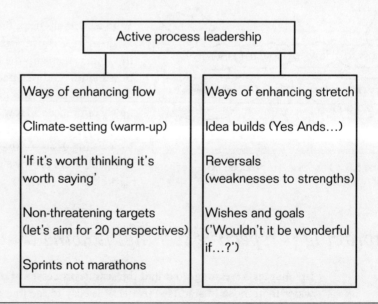

Figure 5.4 Basic ways of enhancing the flow and stretch of perspectives

finding powerful new perspectives are particularly low in untrained groups – lower, for example, than the chances of finding a few unexpected ideas. This is because new perspectives challenge pre-conditions. There may be possibilities for finding a few unexpected ideas, as long as they fit with prevailing perspectives.

For various reasons, a team may be assembled with limited time for climate-building. Some temporary relaxation of criticism can be induced through skilful process leadership. An appropriate practice or warm-up period becomes even more important, providing an opportunity for the process leader to begin the reinforcement of creativity norms. These include reminders of acceptable and unacceptable team practices. 'If it's worth thinking it's worth saying,' is one. 'No clay pigeon shooting,' is another.

One useful tip for inexperienced leaders is to find ways of challenging negativity that do not make the team members fear resentful. Some groups quite enjoy reminders of a humorous kind. Payments to charity seem to be one excellent way of dealing with someone making a negative remark. Even the threat of being 'sin binned' (or 'three strikes and you're out') with the waving of a yellow and then a red card seems better than more censorious ways of administering the feedback.

Another way of encouraging fluency is to set challenging but not threatening targets. Teams will keep going longer if asked to produce a specific number of perspectives or ideas. For inexperienced teams a burst of 10 or 15 perspectives in five minutes is reasonable.

ARE ALL THESE PERSPECTIVES REALLY NECESSARY?

Why should any team need to make a list of 10 or 20 perspectives? The rationale is not immediately obvious. Anyone wishing to involve a team in such a strange activity needs to be sure why the process is worthwhile. For instance, we do not wish to suggest that the perspectives are self-contained sub-problems that have to be dealt with one by one to solve a larger problem.

The reason we emphasize the wide search process is as follows. The team that is in search of a valuable new perspective needs to switch from one way of understanding its situation to another. But the process of switching takes place better as a creative climate builds up – for example in a well-managed brainstorming of How Tos.

The process helps in the 'unfreezing' of team norms. Most experienced practitioners also believe that the suggestions become less anchored in preconceptions as the process develops. The benefits can be appreciated in terms of team process, as well as in terms of the value of the perspectives suggested.

ENCOURAGING A TEAM TO STRETCH FOR NEW PERSPECTIVES

The process leader can encourage stretch by making deliberate appeals or calls for special kinds of perspectives. If the team has been struggling in a motivated but ineffective way to break out of old perspectives, such interventions can induce a rapidly increased flow, which will also have a higher content of stretched ideas. If we refer again to Figure 5.4 we see how Yes Ands, reversals and wishful goals all support the stretch process.

CASCADING INTERVENTIONS MAINTAIN MOMENTUM

The outcome is a process that takes off and receives repeated boosts through the skilled interventions of the process leader. A warm-up intervention will sustain momentum for a while. Then the energy drops. Now may be a good time to remind the team of the merits of building on ideas. In particular a negative remark might be light-heartedly turned into a Yes And by the process leader. Such an invitation to be positive may produce a cascade of Yes Ands to explore aspects of a perspective with particular appeal to the team.

When the energy drops, the leader might ask what the team would really like to achieve in terms of a 'Wouldn't it be wonderful if . . . ?'. Once again a suggestion from one team member may produce that kind of constructive competition in which another team member 'Yes Ands' the 'Wouldn't it be wonderful if . . . ?'. The cascade process is tripped off again.

A typical team session in which flow and stretch occurs is shown in Figure 5.5. The sequence clustered around a particular invitation to stretch the imagination may last no longer than a few minutes. Once again, the running is more in the nature of a sprint than a marathon.

Three tips for developing breakthrough perspectives

Team members can be coached in ways of developing breakthrough perspectives. After a search for perspectives, the team should consider whether they are satisfied with their efforts. Are they too close to conventional thinking? If so, even the techniques have not helped the team and additional methods will need to be tried. Further reflection can take place during a pause before the team moves on to generate ideas. We would consider it time well spent if the team discussed and agrees on the benefits from generating more imaginative How Tos. These discussions strengthen the platform of understanding of the team's own performance.

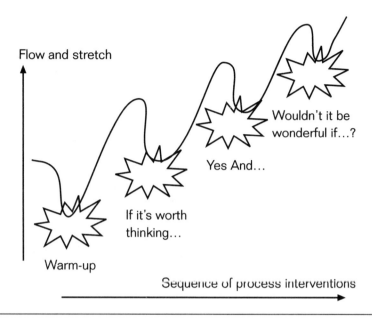

Figure 5.5   Creative interventions for new perspectives

EXAMPLES OF BREAKTHROUGH THINKING TRIGGERED BY 'WOULDN'T IT BE WONDERFUL IF . . . ?' SPECULATION (WIBWI)

These are documented examples of the kind of stretch that produces astonishing breakthroughs. The first is one of the most celebrated examples of breakthrough thinking in the history of innovation. It led to a multi-million dollar instant photography business. The others are all documented examples of the uses of the technique by members of teams that had applied the MPIA approach.

WIBWI this film could be developed in the camera itself? Edwin Land's inspired thinking which led to the Polaroid camera.

WIBWI we could bottle draught Guinness? A suggestion that led Dr Tony Carey to design and patent the Guinness widget, and which eventually led to Canned Draught Guinness.

WIBWI our business had no badly placed offices? Suggested in

a team brainstorming that anticipated the development of computerized banking.

WIBWI our clients could pay for our advertising? Richard Hawksworth, Managing Director of Top Jobs on the Net, hitting on a strategic idea that produced an innovative form of TV advertising.

These three tips are worth trying as a second line of attack. To introduce them at the same time as the other structures for generating perspectives risks technique overload. They are suggestions calling for a conscious effort to switch thinking towards more unexpected, more visual and more positive How Tos.

AIM FOR UNEXPECTED HOW TOS

Previously, the switch to unexpected How Tos was attempted through the 'Wouldn't it be wonderful . . . ?' and 'reversals' techniques of lateral thinking. We would still support the use of these techniques, but after a more considered examination of the persistent themes in the discussion. This should bring into sharper focus the platform of understanding of the dominant How To. Once the team has agreed on the dominant way of seeing the situation, it becomes easier to challenge. In other words, the reversals technique has something to reverse against.

AIM FOR VISUAL HOW TOS

The team can aim for more visual thinking by becoming sensitized to the deficiencies of highly abstract and professional language. Any goal expressed in elite or 'in-group' terms is a candidate for more right-brain thinking. Find a way of bringing the goal to life. Can you express it in a word picture that triggers a visual image in the minds of relative non-experts?

One of our favourite examples came from a team that had trouble finding a new starting-point for ideas. Its professional bias was towards marketing. At first all its discussions had been in terms of market niches and purchasing leverage. The members finally agreed that their usual way of looking at the topic under discussion was 'How to break the generic call'. This is the vocabulary of experienced marketing executives. However, it requires a deep knowledge of consumer behaviour and theories of brand management. As such, it blocks contributions from 'outsiders'.

A young sales representative in the meeting spoke up. 'I don't know this generic call stuff,' he said. 'Is it that the families just walk past our product as if it's not there?'

The impact was electric. The vocabulary changed to a more involving and visual one.

'We could look at how to stand out from the other products,' someone said.

'I wouldn't mind if it was the prime target for hijacking,' someone else commented.

'Wouldn't it be wonderful if we withdrew it, and everybody began asking where it had gone? I'm going somewhere else where they stock it. We could relaunch, on that one.'

And so the breakthrough thinking began. The abstract had become visual and involving.

ENCOURAGE POSITIVE HOW TOS

The existing set of How Tos is examined to see if there is a dominant and persistent emphasis on stopping something unpleasant. The blocking nature of these How Tos can be discussed. Let's look at examples identified as important goals for two different teams. They were both considering the same corporate issue connected with unpleasant publicity assumed to have arisen from an employee talking to the press. The first team took its dominant How To from the spider as

> How to stop employees being disloyal

And followed up with

> How to protect sensitive information from
> being leaked to the press

The second team realized that stopping employees from finding out delicate information might not be as powerful a goal as developing a wider sense of corporate loyalty. It focused its creative efforts on

> How to place information that puts us in a
> good light

And continued with

> How to develop more corporate loyalty

More positive goals are those that engage members of the group and encourage involvement in the changes proposed. As a team develops more positive and involving goals, it is likely to be surrounding itself in a more conducive climate for creativity.

Closing down: learning to live with uncertainties and intuition

One obvious drawback of searching widely is that it calls for unusual measures for closing down or choosing among the perspectives. The fundamental complication is that the decision-making process is dealing with possibilities for future discovery and learning. This involves commitment and a little willingness to try something without the comfort of a solid logical platform of justification. The process is sometimes called intuition, and sometimes 'gut feel'. Intuitive decision-making can produce all kinds of team conflicts. Unsurprisingly, some team members are more comfortable than others with the process.

INTUITION IN SELECTING PERSPECTIVES

The most controversial kind of decision-making draws on the intuition of the team members. Many books have been written on intuition, with some writers considering it to be one of the skills exhibited by great organizational leaders. Other writers emphasize the dangers of such approaches.

Like almost every other controversy, this one is less difficult to deal with if a Both And approach is taken. Intuition is a necessary means of discovering the potential benefits of new perspectives. It may be tested in practice in various ways in order to reduce the concerns that it may be taking the team up a blind alley.

How might intuition be pressed into service? The special climate generated in a creative team seems to encourage people to open up about their intuitions. The dream teams are more open to change and more likely to share intuitions. The more shared the platform of understanding, the more likely there is to be a shared intuition regarding a new perspective. The process fits well into the classical model for creativity. The M-stage involves preparation; the generation of possibilities helps the team to search for a new perspective. If no such perspective emerges, there may well be a period of incubation. The intuitive identification of a new perspective is equivalent to the moment of insight. The validation of the insight is what happens in the action-idea stage.

Time and again we have seen the generation of perspectives enthuse and motivate team members to take on a new perspective. Without such a switch, the outcome is likely to be mundane or standard rather than creative and motivating.

Surrogate intuitions do not work very well. If there is a particular person with responsibility for progressing change – perhaps the client – he or she has to be the one with the new intuition. Sadly, that person may be the most committed to the old perspective, and may have most to lose if things go wrong. Sometimes the other team members become convinced and share an intuition on behalf of the client. This state of affairs may lead to stronger resistance to change from the client.

A variation of this occurs when a team is trying to work on a task for someone not present during the perspective-seeking activity. We have worked with many such teams. All is not lost, but some care has to be taken, as the intuition of a client or sponsor isolated from a team is difficult to anticipate. The team may work thoroughly with information provided and come up with an intuition about what needs to be done. When these intuitive How Tos are taken to the external client, the impact may be low and resistance to change high. The involving climate of the search for new perspectives has been lost somewhere along the way. We will have more to say about this in the next chapter.

Other decision-taking options

Teams may already have preferences for non-intuitive decision processes. We have found that most people we work with believe they already know how to make good decisions. Unfortunately, these beliefs may get in the way of choosing the most promising perspectives.

Our own reading is that those techniques permitting some kind of quantification are most popular as shown in Figure 5.6. Those revealing team consensus rate highly, whereas those in which the team members trust their intuition are least popular. We are often asked what we consider to be the best technique. Our answer is that the specific circumstances will play a part. For perspectives, the weighting methods are not particularly appropriate, as the criteria are not easy to establish in a quantitative way. Voting and clustering have the advantage of helping a team exchange views and, in a minor way, support the building of a platform of understanding. Intuition is generally treated with suspicion, although we believe there are no obvious alternatives when you are examining unclear options.

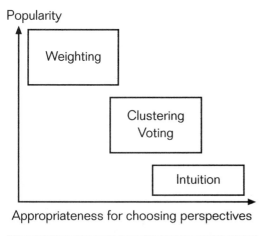

Figure 5.6   Systems for decision-making

LADDERS OF ABSTRACTION

Laddering establishes connections between ends and means, so that the highest ends become located on the top of a ladder which can then be ascended step by step from lower-level means. By highest is meant both most abstracted and most central to absolute human values. The concepts are generated by asking the question 'why' to go up the ladder and 'how' to go down it. Several decades ago this was rediscovered as a management technique. More recently Peter Senge has developed the approach within his famous 'fifth discipline' theory of systems thinking.

The ladder of abstraction can be applied to the perspectives generated in an MPIA exercise. The How Tos can be clustered into any number of levels. Also, any How To can be connected to higher-level How Tos by asking 'why', and split into lesser or lower-level ones by asking the question 'how?' We have found a three-step ladder particularly useful for clustering How Tos as in Figure 5.7. The highest level ones are strategic and generally long term in focus. Once these are examined, the lower-order How Tos become easier to discuss.

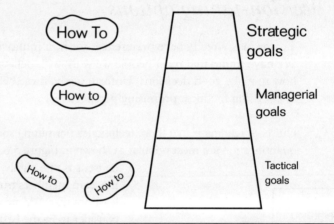

Figure 5.7   Goals grouped by laddering

For a particular team, the balance of How Tos will vary. It is not necessarily correct to assume that strategic goals are best. The 'ownership of the How Tos' will help to indicate where attention is most likely to produce results. In the learning mode that we believe necessary, the team has to ask the question 'Are we mostly concerned here with working at the strategic, managerial or tactical levels?' This sort of questioning will indicate where the team's 'centre of gravity' lies at any given time. Wherever the centre of gravity and location on the ladder, the team will be obliged to move up and down the ladder over the period of the team's existence.

From perspectives to action-ideas

Fresh perspectives point to new ideas. Even a confirmation of confidence in an old perspective may help a team retain momentum. In either case the perspectives stage in MPIA promotes awareness of a team's shared vision and builds on a clarification of its platform of understanding. Through facilitation, the team breaks out of standard ways of perceiving the information in a climate of positivity. Idea-owners emerge and support new breakthrough directions or perspectives. Resilience is strengthened if team members have actively committed to a course of direction. Learning is made easier through the deliberate use of unusual procedures in the MPIA approach.

Perhaps with some help from leadership interventions, teams become stronger in the factors that have been identified as differentiating dream team performance from standard efforts.

Summary

In this chapter we have emphasized that a different way of looking at a situation can lead to breakthrough ideas. The mapping process outlines the terrain and the How To process finds paths through it. How Tos simply transferred from the spider diagram confirm prevailing and persisting mind-sets. If a team sticks very closely to such How Tos, only standard results can be expected. Following the work of Osborn and Parnes, we suggest that teams should seek to improve their perspectives by working on two aspects – flow and stretch.

A switch in perspective indicates that a team has made a significant breakthrough in its appreciation of the varied starting-points available in a complex issue. Its value lies in the implications for future actions and change.

The flow of perspectives can be also encouraged by the Yes And approach and by the deliberate encouragement of a creative climate. Phrases like 'No clay pigeon shooting' remind teams not to evaluate their perspectives too soon. A dream team standard of perspectives can be encouraged by aiming for more unexpected, more visual and more positive How Tos.

Some teams choose a How To intuitively and then have difficulty explaining why. Many managers are suspicious of intuition, feeling more comfortable with structured approaches. A Both And philosophy suggests that an intuitive decision may be tested thoroughly to see whether it is only a distraction.

The more a team shares a platform of understanding, the more it is likely to accept intuitive reactions to the value of a new perspective. Switching perspectives can be one of the most creative steps a team can take. In our enthusiasm for such switches it is important to remember that intuition works best for those experiencing it. A team may misread the impact of an intuition 'for' someone who does not share the team's platform of understanding. This illustrates a crucial point in creative problem-solving: if at all possible, involve the person who needs the new perspectives in the generation of those perspectives. Considerable ingenuity is often needed to make this happen, and sometimes it isn't possible. It pays handsome dividends, however, when it does.

In conclusion, creativity at the P-stage involves decision-making that favours intuition, because more rational approaches fail under conditions of speculation and uncertainty. The selection of a How To is a form of creative sense-making, especially if the new How To is recognized as replacing a previously dominant, but unproductive, How To.

6 PUTTING ACTION INTO IDEAS AND IDEAS INTO ACTION

TAG teams in action

A whole generation of TV viewers has been brought up on the colourful spectacle of professional wrestling. One of the versions involves TAG teams. The contest combines show business, athleticism, ferocity and teamwork. There are rules, but these seem to be creatively interpreted, and the referee is as likely to be a casualty as members of the TAG teams. The characterizing feature of a TAG contest is that a member of the team brings their partner into play by touching or tagging. Once tagged, the partner immediately leaps into action. The other partner is at that moment supposed to leave the wrestling ring.

The TAG wrestlers epitomize the two interconnected themes of this chapter. How might teams become more action-oriented in their ideas? And how might the action-oriented ideas increase the chances of achieving outstanding team results? We will suggest that the way forward is also to do with TAG teams, although our use of the term has nothing to do with wrestling. It refers to the Thought-Action Gap.

Overview

Many assumptions about change lead to a wide gap between thought and action. The combination of ideas and actions within the MPIA approach ensures that teams develop ideas through action-oriented mind-sets. An illustration of this is given from a system of new product development. Each idea is examined primarily from the action mind-set of rapid conversion of an idea into a product in a bottle. Two approaches are suggested within the MPIA framework for generating more powerful action ideas. The first approach uses lateral thinking methods. The second is based on the deliberate application of metaphoric thinking. Both help teams escape from the barriers sometimes imposed if they stick too closely to their platform of understanding. In the final section of the chapter, we will look at selection procedures that are most in keeping with creative team behaviours.

Connecting ideas to actions: narrowing the thought-action gap

The thought-action gap constitutes a persistent difficulty encountered in schemes to improve human behaviours, and is often described as putting theory into practice. In schemes that are presented as sequences of stages, the thought-action gap is often hinted at, but left unstated. For example, many problem-solving systems end with some kind of action stage. The implication is 'get the thinking sorted out, and then you can start worrying about action'. Typical rational models of problem-solving end with the stages of solution-finding (thought) followed by a stage of acceptance-finding or implementation (action).

Less formally, the thought-action gap is hinted at in the often-related anecdote about hare soup. If you read the cookery book, preparing hare soup is simply a matter of following the instructions. 'First catch your hare,' the recipe begins. Only when would-be cooks begin the action do they become aware of the gap between the thought of making hare soup and the action of catching your hare.

There are rather complex reasons why the thought-action gap can never be totally overcome. What can be done, however, is to find ways of managing and reducing the difficulties resulting from the gap. Our proposal is to boost the number of ideas with strong action implications.

Figure 6.1 introduces the MPIA in three formats. The simple format represents the four stages of mapping, perspectives, ideas and actions as if they were completely distinct. The standard and boosted versions have three stages, because ideas and actions are treated as a single stage. In simple, standard, and boosted version alike, each stage involves a 'search widely' or divergent component, and a 'choose wisely' or convergent component.

The simple version is perfectly adequate for learning the various techniques within the stages. However, we believe that the behaviours of most teams are more accurately represented by the standard and boosted versions. The standard version is what tends to be found in the activities of standard teams. Ideas are generated, which may have no obvious actions implied. These are shown as $I(-)$ ideas. A few ideas have rather weak actions implied. These are shown as $I(a)$ ideas.

Teams that have been trained to develop action-ideas behave as shown in

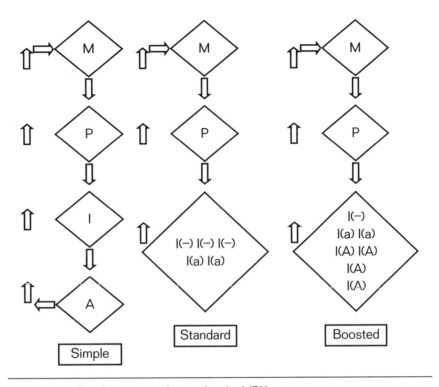

Figure 6.1 Enriching action-ideas within the MPIA system

the boosted version. There are fewer I(−) and I(a) ideas. Instead, the teams generate strongly action-oriented ideas shown as I(A)s.

In this chapter we consider ways of boosting the proportion of action-ideas through interventions such as the use of creativity-triggers. We have found two particularly powerful ways of achieving this. The first ensures that the outputs of idea generation are more deliberately and consciously connected with action steps. The actions are brought into the thoughts, so that the thoughts can be more easily brought into action. In its simple form this is the product-in-a-bottle concept. The second approach seeks to boost the ideas beyond those that the team would find if it remains too close to its prevailing platform of understanding.

The product-in-a-bottle concept

Some years ago, an industrial chemist working for a chemicals organization put forward a powerful way of turning ideas into action. The chemist's name was John Carson, and he was subsequently to become an internationally-known figure for his approaches to creating new products and new businesses.

He called his first idea-generation approach the Scimitar system. The term stood for systematic creativity using integrative modelling. The basic idea was that innovation is best stimulated by assembling a cross-disciplinary team that would engage in a systematic search process for new ideas. That was the systematic creativity. The search involved an examination of all the raw materials used by the company, all the processes for transforming the raw materials and all the markets into which the end products were sold. This search was conducted by constructing a three-dimensional box. One axis was allocated to the raw materials, the second axis to the processes and the final axis to markets. Then each existing product of the company was identified with a specific location in the box, according to raw materials, processes and markets connected with the product. New ideas were generated by systematic examination of the gaps in the box or 'cube-crawling'.

In the original setting of a chemicals company, the teams were told to give priority to ideas that they could convert into a product in a bottle. Specifically, at the end of a team session, all ideas were rated for action possibilities. Then the team members divided up the ideas among themselves. Everyone was required to turn each idea into tangible form for the next ideas meeting (perhaps within a period of one month).

Scimitar was to prove its worth in a wide range of companies for which new product ideas were developed. It remains one of the most ingenious ways for supporting what is now known as incremental or continuous improvement innovations.

If we express Scimitar in the vocabulary of MPIA (as in Figure 6.2), we see that

> The three-dimensional company box is the map of the territory.
> Each smaller box is a perspective.
> Each perspective is used as a starting point for ideas.
> Each idea is converted into an action-idea (product in a bottle).

In discussion, the basic idea would quickly be developed with considerations of what steps might be needed to produce a tangible prototype. The remarkable feature of the Scimitar approach was the impressive way that

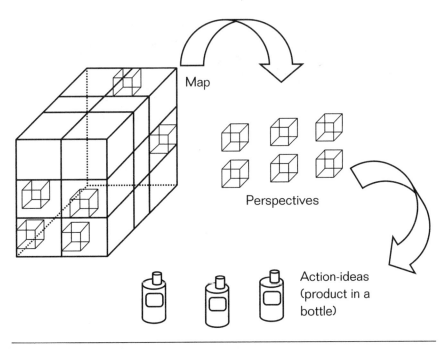

Figure 6.2 The original Scimitar approach for producing action-ideas (product in a bottle)

ideas were converted into products in bottles. It is this feature of the system that we believe could be studied and applied in a far wider range of creative team activities.

Stated more generally, the product-in-a-bottle approach reduces the thought-action gap. It is that general concept that we have borrowed and expanded for the I-A stage of the MPIA creative team approach.

Skilled leaders are adept at ways of encouraging a team to think of more action-oriented ideas. The approach can be seen in Figure 6.3 in which team members create mental pictures or 'action movies' as the starting-point for their own mental show. Perhaps the team initially produced mostly standard ideas of the I(−) and a few of the I(a) kind. The leader may ask a question such as 'So how would you see yourself doing that?' when an idea is suggested. The subsequent efforts are more action-oriented and more ideas of an I(A) kind are developed.

If the ideas are suggested as word pictures, team members are likely to be able to identify with them more strongly. The most energizing ideas are 'we'-focused rather than 'you'- or 'they'-focused. One of the advantages of

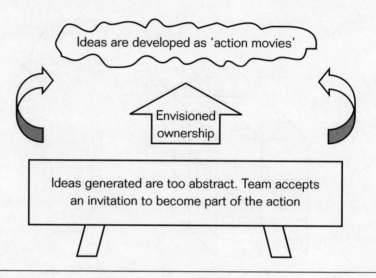

Figure 6.3   How envisioned ownership creates action-ideas

'we' pictures is that the participants experience a more supportive climate. Even if the team members are working to a How To proposed by a client, the most promising ideas still paint a picture in which the client 'sees' he or she is not alone. The creative team is one in which some responsibility for shared actions is recognized.

To summarize, a focus on action-ideas can give a creative team a helpful mind-set which triggers involving and energizing ideas. This overcomes one of the common weaknesses of simple idea-generation meetings, namely a set of ideas that are hard to implement. In other words, the connection of ideas to actions reduces the thought-action gap.

Beyond standard ideas: two additional creativity specials

Action-ideas tend to be more useful than ideas with a wide thought-action gap. Integrating action into ideas is a necessary step to achieving creative results in a team. However, it is not the only step. The team still has to develop action-ideas that make a difference. In particular, there is a need for ways of going beyond the obvious ideas that most standard teams are likely to come up with. We will take a closer look at how lateral-thinking and metaphoric processes can play a part in transforming the quality and novelty of ideas. In practice, the development of action-ideas and breakthrough ideas may take place at the same time. The common starting-point is a reflection on the set of ideas produced.

THE INVITATION TO BREAK AWAY FROM THE PLATFORM OF UNDERSTANDING

The creative team has generated a range of ideas. Let's suppose it used the MPIA system, so that the ideas followed a mapping and perspective-seeking stage. The result has been a set of ideas that seem too close to previously known ones. Perhaps the meeting has resulted in 'business as usual'. Sometimes all best efforts result in what might be called a brain dump, rather than a brainstorm! The experienced leader reviews the ideas with the rest of the team. If there is general agreement that the ideas are too close to past thinking, the leader may suggest the use of some blockbusting techniques as in Figure 6.4.

LATERAL THINKING: THE RANDOM JOLT TECHNIQUE

We tend to begin the breakthrough efforts with the lateral thinking techniques mentioned in Chapter 5. These are relatively easy to introduce to teams without a great deal of training. However, there are a few more powerful techniques that also appeal to teams willing to try them.

The random jolt technique – mentioned in Chapter 3 and shown in Figure 3.3 – works by forcing the team to switch attention away from its topic of main interest.

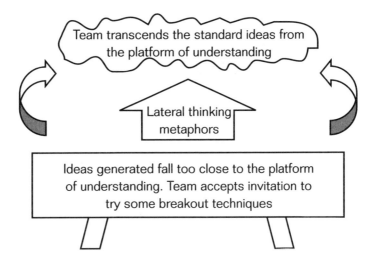

Figure 6.4   How breakthrough ideas are produced

We work with a much-cherished 'prop' – a white plastic globe fitted with a transparent plastic window. There are about 3000 words, each on small cards, in the globe. Random words can be displayed in the window by a team member shaking the globe and reading out the first word that comes into view. The rest of the team has to react to the word and connect it with a perspective that has been selected for idea generation.

The ritual of globe-shaking has the additional effect of involving the quieter team members in a shared experience. The 'prop' helps break with the more cognitive (left-brain) mind-set of teams following their standard work patterns. We often find that after being introduced to the technique, a team member will seek us out during subsequent idea sessions to borrow the globe.

The globe is not a necessity, and may be replaced by any of a host of other ways of dramatizing the production of a random word or image. For instance, it has been successfully replaced with a dictionary or with a set of words of the kind shown in Figure 6.5.

The most successful teams seem able to incorporate the words into an emotionally involving stream of thought. We have found a good

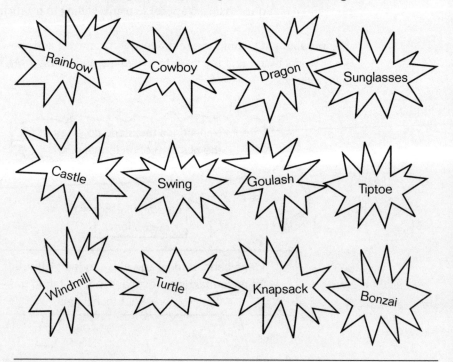

Figure 6.5   Trigger words for breakthrough ideas

THE BENEFITS OF BREAKTHROUGH THINKING

In training we like to start with an exercise on finding ideas that improve a taken-for-granted object, ideally one that is part of the team's working environment. This gives the exercise a level of necessary realism. After this 'warm-up', we invite the team to apply the same technique to real work issues.

With a reasonable willingness on the part of the team to try new techniques, the approaches have a good chance of delivering ideas that had not been thought of at the start of the exercise. We kept records of results from such exercises over a period of years and found that between 30 and 50 per cent of the efforts were rated as producing at least one idea new to the participants after half an hour of practice.

arrangement is to encourage smaller groups of two or three team members to build a shared idea around a supplied word. The experience need only last a few minutes. The less successful teams seem more reluctant to 'go with the flow'. In those circumstances, their process is noticeably left brain, with little evidence that the team is being swept up into a more intense creative mood.

One further hint for team leaders: some members become over-concerned about being able to come up with spectacularly different ideas during lateral thinking exercises. This can even inhibit contributions, because there is less willingness to be open with other teams members about their first ideas.

These are circumstances in which the leader should remind team members of the more general rule of creative thinking – 'If it's worth thinking it's worth saying.' Then the Yes And approach can be put to work, perhaps to add actions to some of the ideas that have too wide a thought-action gap.

METAPHOR: MAKING THE FAMILIAR STRANGE AND THE STRANGE FAMILIAR

Visions, right-brain thinking and perhaps metaphor are popularly associated with the act of creation. We see the application of metaphor as a means of bringing together two different mind-sets. The first is the dominant and often professional mind-set, which has influenced previous thinking. This tends to be an economic mind-set for business problems, or a technical mind-set for engineering problems, and so on. We might see the mind-set as an important contribution to the platform of understanding of any experienced team with shared backgrounds.

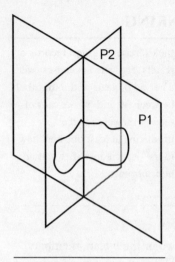

Figure 6.6 The two mind-sets of a metaphor

The second mind-set is any opposing one that both connects with the first and helps the team escape from some of its assumptions. It tends to be more visual and engaging and is one that reaches out and involves many who would not understand the many aspects of professional know-how connected with the dominant mind-set. This is the mind-set that makes the familiar strange, until the familiar and strange merge into a powerful new idea. Arthur Koestler describes this as a 'bisociation of mental planes' (as shown in Figure 6.6).

Over time, we have developed an approach that inexperienced teams have found easy to follow. The perspective should be one that has been identified as promising for breakthrough thinking. Evocative perspectives that already trigger right-brain imagery are best (see Chapter 4). The team spends a little time looking for a way of thinking about the perspective in a way which is very different from their usual professional approach.

Let's see how this worked in a real-life example involving a European-based team of technical professionals. The team was experiencing a skills shortage of a highly specialized kind. Its immediate methods of recruitment had been of no avail. The MPIA approach had helped the team to focus on a perspective, which had been stated as:

> How to attract a top-flight electronics specialist into the team.

The technique involves the team in finding and writing down the metaphorical How To on the left side of a wall chart or flip chart as shown in Figure 6.7. Ideas for dealing with the metaphor are then generated. Finally, the team turns to the right side of the chart and begins to find connections between the metaphor and the problem in its traditionally expressed format.

In the example, the professional mind-set had been translated into 'How to attract rare birds to our garden'. About a dozen ideas were quickly produced. These were then reworked to give new ideas for the actual problem. Our own recollections are that the basis of some of the ideas was quite new to the team. Other ideas, although already considered, were re-examined in a more considered way during the metaphor exercise. The team had no trouble agreeing action-ideas and eventually recruited their 'rare bird'.

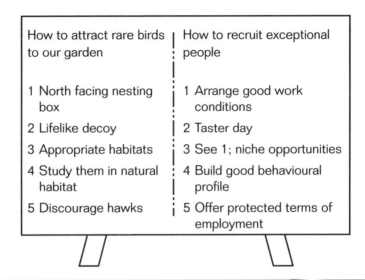

How to attract rare birds to our garden	How to recruit exceptional people
1 North facing nesting box	1 Arrange good work conditions
2 Lifelike decoy	2 Taster day
3 Appropriate habitats	3 See 1; niche opportunities
4 Study them in natural habitat	4 Build good behavioural profile
5 Discourage hawks	5 Offer protected terms of employment

Figure 6.7   A simple metaphoric method

This introduction to metaphor is a fitting place to conclude our account of approaches for generating breakthrough ideas. We would not want to suggest that a team will always find a metaphor that will make a difference. On the contrary, the skills involved in finding powerful metaphors develop with practice and experience. We believe the investment of time in developing these skills to be greatly worthwhile. After all, any given way of seeing the world can be re-expressed in vivid metaphoric terms. By that we mean that metaphors can be found offering promise for idea breakthroughs for any technical or organizational problem. Furthermore, if a team can collectively come up with some candidate metaphors, the most promising often win instant acclaim. Such an intuitive team assessment is also often confirmed when the metaphor is explored more deeply.

The closing-down process

CLOSING DOWN CAN BE CREATIVE

A common assumption is that opening-up or divergent processes are creative and that closing-down or convergent processes are not. This view is reinforced in writings on decision-taking in which the search side is linked with brainstorming, for example. Even in books on creativity techniques, the reader might be left with the impression that all the creative efforts occur at the divergent stage of the process. We prefer to regard both processes as creative in their different ways.

Decision-taking is indeed often approached in a way which excludes creativity. Yet, as we will show, there are ways of building creativity into convergent processes. This requires the team to operate in an open-minded way that treats the decisions as mechanisms for exploring possibilities not as rules that eliminate possibilities. Overall, the creative approach is one in which the design provides good opportunities for learning. We will shortly see how this can come about.

TECHNIQUES FOR SELECTING IDEAS

Selecting which ideas to develop is never a simple process. The various approaches remain those that had value in selecting perspectives, as shown in Figure 5.6. However, the appropriateness of the techniques now shifts somewhat as shown in Figure 6.8.

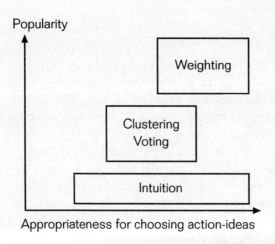

Figure 6.8 Selection processes for action-ideas

We suggested that decision processes based on weighting were rather unsatisfactory when applied to selecting How Tos. They are more valuable, however, when a team is examining a shortlist of action-ideas. Clustering and voting still have the merits of encouraging discussion among team members (a help to building a platform of understanding). Intuition has fewer claims to be the 'only show in town' as the context of the decisions has become closer to the empirical world of products and processes (remember the product-in-a-bottle ideal for new ideas). In these circumstances, intuition can be supported by more analytical approaches which we will now examine.

THE CRITERION MATRIX APPROACH

The criterion matrix approach using quantitative criteria is one that finds the greatest appeal among professional teams. The process of studying the ideas carefully and debating the criteria happens to be a good way for team members to reveal their beliefs and assumptions. Furthermore, the process can be made public. For many teams this is a necessary precaution as they may be called upon to justify what they are doing. A well-documented

THE QUANTITATIVE CRITERION MATRIX

1 Reduce the numbers of ideas to a convenient shortlist. This is not difficult, even without quantitative methods!

2 Generate criteria, taking care that these are not overlapping or ambiguous. A set of between five and eight criteria is both convenient and effective. Typically these will contain a criterion of cost or cost/benefit; one of technical feasibility; one of time constraints; one of acceptability; one of 'potential for knock-on adverse effects'; one of novelty. The set may have some criteria specific to the kinds of ideas evaluated.

3 Discuss the criteria as a team, seeking to arrive at consensus on their relative importance. Give each criterion a weight from one to ten.

4 Examine each idea across all the criteria. Reach a consensus of the value of each idea for all criteria again using a one-to-ten scale.

5 Arrive at a weighted score for each idea.

This quantified method of rating ideas can be found in numerous texts on decision analysis and problem-solving. We endorse it for two reasons.

It can be used to make the decision-making process transparent. It can also promote debate and learning about the decision-takers' platform of understanding. On the debit side, we have found the process hopelessly inadequate for dealing with the non-rational processes that go on in teams. It is also lengthy and can be contentious. Furthermore, the weighted figures give a dangerous but spurious impression of accuracy.

Figure 6.9 shows an example of the quantitative criterion matrix in use for evaluating diversification prospects for a multinational organization.

account of their evaluation processes may even protect them from less reasoned judgements by influential outsiders.

The quantitative criterion matrix process is shown above. We have assumed that the ideas have already been generated in considerable numbers.

Despite its widespread popularity we believe the weighted criterion matrix to be most appropriate when the basis of judgement is mostly on technical criteria that can easily be quantified. It works relatively well for selecting among a shortlist of computer systems, for example. It is less effective for selecting novel ideas. For that we prefer a qualitative version as shown overleaf, which also happens to be more amenable to a creative decision-making process.

	Flair 4	Global reach 9	PR 3	Innovation 9	Technology 6
Youth	36	81	18	54	42
Leisure	28	81	21	63	42
Oil	16	90	12	54	48
Consumer	24	81	24	63	48
Retail	32	36	15	81	48
IT	28	81	15	81	54

Figure 6.9   Criterion matrix: quantitative version

THE QUALITATIVE CRITERION MATRIX

1 Reduce the ideas to an acceptable shortlist.
2 Generate criteria as in the quantitative approach.
3 Use a non-quantitative coding system to examine the value of the ideas. We recommend a+ for a more acceptable than a less acceptable idea; a− for a less acceptable rather than more acceptable idea; and a? for ideas which do not fit easily into either + or − categories.

The skilled facilitator seeks permission at the outset to speed up the process whenever there is disagreement. She or he will do this by allocating a ? to any cell for which consensus cannot be reached within one minute. This approach quickly reveals the most promising ideas. The team always has the opportunity to improve any of the front-runners within the time constraints of the exercise.

4 The team also has the option of reconstructing the matrix by modifying the criteria if the result seems counter-intuitive.

The application of the ? convention is one of the most important aspects of the qualitative approach. Rather than debate lengthily, the team can be swiftly moved on, having recorded their lack of consensus with the ?

Once the matrix is complete, the team examines the pattern of +s, −s and ?s. The time taken over this is rather more dependent on the prevailing circumstances but a time limit is best set at the beginning of the process.

A column totally made up of <+> ratings or a column of <−> ratings indicates that the criterion applied has no discriminating effect for the ideas examined. The criterion can be dropped from the examination or it may be the focus for a discussion aimed at sharpening the criterion itself. For example, a column rated all <+> on 'easy to implement' may be reappraised against the criterion 'can implement completely in six months'.

A row with a complete set of <+> ratings is the signal for a very promising idea. On the other hand, if almost all the rows have <+> ratings, the experienced facilitator may suspect that the team is perhaps prone to wishful thinking.

Figure 6.10 shows an example of the qualitative criterion matrix in use for evaluating diversification prospects for a multinational organization.

The most usual application of a criterion matrix is with weighted criteria, as indicated above. It may be necessary for a team to be confronted with the rationale for creative decision-making before examining the qualitative approach. The immediate objections sometimes raised are indications of a dominant mind-set in favour of quantification. This is why some prior discussion is valuable. For most people, the objections do not persist once the method has been demonstrated.

The speed of the process contrasts with experiences the team members may have had with quantitative approaches. The use of the question mark is a

	Flair	Global reach	PR	Innovation	Technology
Youth	+	+	?	+	+
Leisure	+	+	?	+	+
Oil	−	+	−	?	+
Consumer	?	+	?	+	?
Retail	?	−	?	+	+
IT	?	+	−	+	+

Figure 6.10   Criterion matrix: qualitative version

wonderfully simple way of keeping the meeting moving forward. Note also that the qualitative approach leads more naturally to a discussion and learning process among team members. The team cannot be accused of 'putting itself at the mercy of dubious numbers'.

OTHER DECISION PROCESSES AND THEIR CREATIVE MANAGEMENT

Some readers may have noticed a 'first catch your hare' or thought-action gap within the description above of evaluating ideas through a criterion matrix. At the outset, we suggested that the matrix method is particularly effective for a shortlist of ideas. Yet a systematic effort at generating ideas will easily produce 50 to 100 ideas. Other decision processes are therefore needed in order to achieve a shortlist. We will outline the primary practical applications we have found for the main decision systems and our efforts at managing the process in a creative way.

Faced with 100 ideas from a creative team, the simplest method is to make a preliminary sort into the 'old hat' ideas and the others. Old hat ideas are those that have no evidence of novelty in the context of the meeting. This eliminates up to 90 per cent of the ideas if brainstorming rules have been applied. Even if the ideas come from more conventional sources, up to 60 per cent of the ideas may well fall into the old hat category. Nothing particularly creative so far!

Working with the smaller set of promising ideas, we would then invite the team members to nominate those they would be prepared to work with personally. This first stage is a kind of 'include me in' voting which identifies action champions.

Stage two is for the team to reflect on the willingness of members to take on ideas. In discussion it becomes possible to identify ways that individuals can be supported so as to put more into their group contributions. This is a mechanism for learning about team behaviours and motivation as well as for reaching decisions. A criterion matrix on a shortened list of acceptable ideas can then be applied to indicate their relative merits.

Another approach for reducing numbers of ideas is to build up groupings or

THE DANGERS OF FALSE INTUITION

In the development of new perspectives we were rather positive about the role of intuition. In this way a sense that a particular viewpoint had been underexamined could be followed up with a search for new and unexpected ideas. The risk of a false intuition – the ideas do not fulfil the dream – is low, and the intuition can be abandoned with little investment.

In the selection of action-ideas, intuition may still be encouraged. However, because these are deliberately related to actions, intuition is now more likely to lead to rapid actions and associated costs. Teams can be swept up into what is called the risky shift mode of behaving.

This is the dilemma facing the creative team leader. We have repeatedly emphasized the importance of encouraging enthusiasm and commitment and no team leader wants to kill the momentum that can be generated by individual hunches. We would argue that the danger lies not in taking the risk of trusting an intuition; nor does it lie in the rapid implementation of ideas in the absence of hard evidence. Rather, the danger occurs if a team is carried along by the motivating promise of a false vision under the impression that it has reached the decision in a more reasoned fashion. As has been found in several other contexts, the creative team has to find a Yes And resolution of the dilemma. The team that learns from its own behaviours and studies its platform of understanding is likely to be more aware of its intuitive impulses. As a consequence it knows how to take action when evidence starts building up that the intuition is leading the team into trouble. The watchword becomes intuition and openness for signals that fresh thinking and actions are required.

clusters. The famous Post-it® Notes (also valued as a map-building aid) can be easily moved around to reveal families of closely related ideas. We have noticed that some teams concentrate on producing a small number of 'big ideas' which are labels for the clusters. These tend to be abstractions which conceal the directness and uniqueness of a few of the most potent of the smaller ideas and are likely to have lost much of their action character. As a team facilitator you might consider using the clustering technique to identify search areas. The clusters can then be subjected to our old friend the criterion matrix approach. The results from such a matrix analysis can indicate how a portfolio of action-ideas might be assembled to take into account the rated value of the territories (clusters) and the benefits of a widely spread portfolio of ideas.

Summary

In this chapter we have emphasized the importance of eliminating the TAG – the Thought-Action Gap – between ideas and actions. The gap between theory and practice bedevils many organizational initiatives and idea generation can suffer in the same way.

The thought-action gap can never be totally overcome, but we suggest ways in which it can be managed. When teams are generating ideas, there will be some with actions clearly implied. We encourage a deliberate effort to boost the number of ideas of this kind.

Particularly powerful ways of boosting ideas are the product-in-a-bottle approach, a lateral thinking random jolt and metaphor. The product in a bottle, derived from the Scimitar system propounded by John Carson, encourages consideration of what would be needed to turn the idea into a prototype.

A lateral thinking jolt provides the stimulus of more unusual ideas for a team that has stuck too close to its platform of understanding. We suggest a jolt in the form of a random word. The most successful teams seem able to incorporate the words into an emotionally involving stream of thought.

Metaphor is a means of bringing together two different mind-sets, the professional or dominant mind-set and a more visual mind-set from another domain. This helps the team escape from some of its assumptions by 'making the familiar strange, and the strange familiar'. The ideas produced by this process often yield a richer set of starting points for action.

Choosing ideas is as creative a process as generating them. Creativity can be built into the choice process by treating the decisions as mechanisms for exploring possibilities not as rules that eliminate possibilities. We demonstrate the criteria matrix for choosing ideas in both a quantitative and qualitative way.

To develop a short list of ideas grouping or clustering round a theme can help. Care needs to be taken that the team does not focus on a small number of 'big ideas' which are labels for the clusters. When this happens the ideas lose much of their action character.

Intuition has a place in the selection process. It can be strengthened if the team continues to apply monitoring of the outcomes of actions. Otherwise the intuition may lead to what has been termed the risky shift mode of behaviour.

Postscript

Some years ago a jumbo jet hit a freak tropical storm while flying high over Eastern Asia. The violence virtually disabled the controls. After an agonizing descent to the nearest airport the plane approached the runway. The emergency services were braced for a disaster. Yet the crippled plane landed safely and with remarkably few injuries. At the subsequent press conference, the pilot was asked how he had been able to carry out virtually unheard-of manoeuvres and get every thing right first time. The pilot explained: 'It was the first time I had done it in action, but I had done similar things a lot of times in mental rehearsal.'

This is a wonderful lesson for all of us. We can improve if we practise. But for the unexpected, we can still practise in our imagination. In the next three chapters we have collected together a whole set of examples of teams in action. We can benefit from the cases by that sort of mental rehearsal. If you want to try it, we suggest you read the accounts, imagining yourself inside the action. Afterwards you can recall what happened, and how it might be applied to your own circumstances. Then we suggest you carry out a second mental rehearsal, this time making something happen in your imagination that moves you towards one of your own goals.

PART *III*

CREATIVE TEAMS IN ACTION

We have based the ideas in this book on teams engaged in innovation work, teams operating in networks and teams applying the MPIA or related systems. Chapter 7 deals with innovation teams in action. Chapter 8 looks at networks of teams in action. Chapter 9 concentrates on project teams in action.

In Chapter 7 the teams were found within large and small companies, some of which applied directly deliberate structuring techniques related to the MPIA system. Others did not. We will be concentrating on the characteristics of dream teams engaged in innovative tasks.

In Chapter 8, the focus shifts to the challenges of individuals and teams engaged in networking activities. Here we will look more closely at the structures and approaches used for network activation.

Chapter 9 contains examples of project teamwork. The characteristic of the cases is a sponsor or client who is supported through the efforts of a project team trained in the MPIA system.

In all three chapters, we are looking for ways of reinforcing the principles of teamwork covered in the first two parts of the book.

7 INNOVATION TEAMS IN ACTION

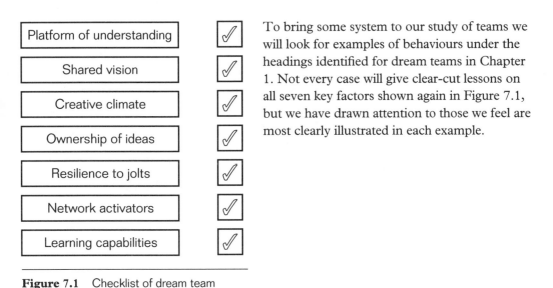

Platform of understanding	✓
Shared vision	✓
Creative climate	✓
Ownership of ideas	✓
Resilience to jolts	✓
Network activators	✓
Learning capabilities	✓

To bring some system to our study of teams we will look for examples of behaviours under the headings identified for dream teams in Chapter 1. Not every case will give clear-cut lessons on all seven key factors shown again in Figure 7.1, but we have drawn attention to those we feel are most clearly illustrated in each example.

Figure 7.1 Checklist of dream team characteristics

The Klea innovation: achievement at the speed of light

'Achieving things at the speed of light.' That was the challenge set to the ICI Fluorochemical technical team at the beginning of 1987. More than 60 chemists, chemical engineers and chemical plant designers worked non-stop with outside contractors to develop and produce ICI's replacement for Chlorofluorocarbons (CFCs), marketed as KLEA 134a. A unique combination of environmental and political pressure produced an equally unique situation – to replace a business developed over 60 years with a complete new range of products in less than ten years. It can take 17 years and literally millions of pounds to research and market a new compound; the ICI Fluorochemical team had five years and 50 million pounds to achieve their goal.

CFCs had been implicated in the thinning of the ozone layer first reported in

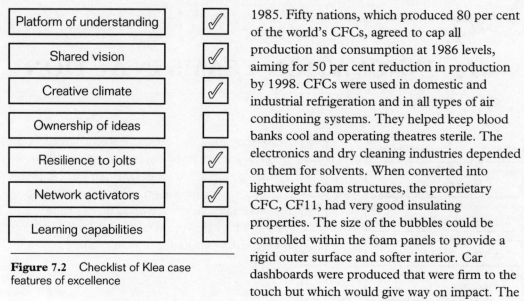

Platform of understanding	✓
Shared vision	✓
Creative climate	✓
Ownership of ideas	
Resilience to jolts	✓
Network activators	✓
Learning capabilities	

Figure 7.2   Checklist of Klea case features of excellence

1985. Fifty nations, which produced 80 per cent of the world's CFCs, agreed to cap all production and consumption at 1986 levels, aiming for 50 per cent reduction in production by 1998. CFCs were used in domestic and industrial refrigeration and in all types of air conditioning systems. They helped keep blood banks cool and operating theatres sterile. The electronics and dry cleaning industries depended on them for solvents. When converted into lightweight foam structures, the proprietary CFC, CF11, had very good insulating properties. The size of the bubbles could be controlled within the foam panels to provide a rigid outer surface and softer interior. Car dashboards were produced that were firm to the touch but which would give way on impact. The low boiling-points, non-flammability and non-toxicity of CFC11 and CFC12 made them ideal propellants for aerosols – probably the use best known to the public – such as hairsprays and home cleaning products. In addition, CFCs made many medical treatments possible, such as treating asthma by inhaler.

By the mid-1980s, a range of comforts of modern life had been greatly enhanced by CFCs and various businesses within ICI depended on supplying such products. So the race to develop CFC substitutes was on. In 1987 a project team was set up to replace ICI's CFCs with Hydrofluoroalkanes (HFAs).

The different HFAs are created by chemical reactions in which the chlorine atoms in a CFC are partly or totally eliminated by substituting hydrogen atoms. The new products degrade harmlessly in the atmosphere. However, individual HFAs had to be developed to match the required applications. Air conditioning a car, for example, usually requires that the temperature drop to a comfortable level within a few seconds. For a building a constant, less dramatic and longer lasting temperature drop is required.

Hugo Steven, Research and Development Manager of the New Fluorochemicals Team was associated with the project from its inception to its commercialization four years later. For most of those working on the project, it was the first time they had been involved in this type of development and it raised some interesting issues. This is the experience in Hugo's words.

'IT CAN'T BE DONE'

The first really big thing was the time scale. Four years is a very short time in which to develop and produce a product and to build a plant. We had to battle with the notion that it couldn't be done. We also had to work differently. Rachel Spooncer, the chemical engineer responsible for plant design, was involved with the chemists' work from the very beginning. She asked some very detailed questions. At first the chemists were a bit surprised; they were accustomed to working out plant design issues after the chemistry had been developed. Answering questions like 'What happens if the heater fails or the pressure drops?' early on meant that the plant could be modified at the design stage, saving time and expense later. Rachel was also key in establishing the empowered working culture.

We had to manage a huge risk element. The second-generation plant was being designed before the first one was fully operational; we had to have faith in what we were doing and communicate that to the business managers funding us. We were going to the board for sanction for the second plant before we knew the first one would work. For the first-generation plant we used a technique called 'visionary flowsheeting'. We called everyone together, the chemists, process engineers, vessel specialists, and asked them to imagine what the plant would look like. We got a picture in our minds and worked from there. We also appointed the plant manager right at the beginning of the project, so he knew that any decision we made, he would have to implement.

From the very beginning we stressed the special nature of the team. We were located in a separate building and even the business manager couldn't get in without letting us know he was coming – he didn't have the combination for the door! We wanted people to feel that they were protected from worrying about what would happen if they failed. It was important that everyone should feel part of the same thing. People had different reasons for wanting to belong to the project. Some wanted the opportunity to be first to market; some wanted to save the planet; others wanted the opportunity to do some really exciting chemistry. Whatever their initial motivation, we worked to make them feel part of a cohesive team. We had open-plan offices to help people talk to each other and a very flat organizational structure. If anyone had a problem to deal with they often solved it by walking around and chatting to other people. During the development phase, an engineer solved a key chemical problem, and an engineering bottleneck was dealt with by a chemist! The way we tried to encourage dialogue certainly paid off.

It was not only internally that teamwork counted. The team worked closely with customers because adjustments had to be made to the systems in which the HFAs function. The test team ran parallel tests with major customers to discuss the modifications necessary to their equipment. Once the plant was designed, external contractors worked closely with the company to make sure the plant was built within time and to budget. The enterprise drew on the skills of vessel design and mechanical engineers, control systems experts and hazard advisers. Maintaining the energy and momentum of the project was one of Hugo Steven's main tasks.

DEADLINES, DEADLINES, DEADLINES

We knew we were up against a very tight deadline. In circumstances like that you have to work to keep setbacks in perspective. You also have to be careful that people don't work too hard, get burned out and then you lose them. In the beginning most of us weren't used to working across functional lines. None of us knew what to expect. But we kept the main goals of the project very much in mind and we celebrated our achievements. For instance, Dick Powell, who ran the applications lab found a problem with HFA 134a as a refrigerant. A compressor needs an oil for its moving metal components. HFA 134a won't mix with the mineral oil previously used for pumping the refrigerant through the compressor and the system. The materials separated out into two very distinct layers. We tested many things and eventually found that the chemicals in brake fluid would do the job! We had to keep going until we found an answer.

Tony Ryan worked on synthesis routes for some of the other HFAs. ICI intends to develop HFAs for other markets such as polyurethane and polystyrene foam-blowing. HFAs are also intended for refrigerants for chillers for cooling water, ice-making machines, butchers' cold rooms, and any other applications requiring temperatures around $-40°C$. His job included ways of maximizing yield and optimizing the product selectivity. He was told which compounds appeared most suitable and it was up to him to find the best routes to use them.

At the start there was a brainstorming session. For one of the compounds we had over 100 routes suggested – some well known, some off the wall. We drew up a list of criteria, including raw materials available, by-products made, technical feasibility, and so on. We made some decisions and then got on with the job. Action was really important and we prided ourselves on being able to get together the right equipment quickly. If something didn't work, we'd say, OK, let's go for something else.

A team member stuck a picture up where they had to
pass it every day. The caption said 'This car needs
134a by 1 January 1991'

Figure 7.3   Klea's vision

One of the development team was a car
fanatic. One day he brought in a picture of a
high-performance, air-conditioned car and
stuck it up at the entrance to the building.
Above it he wrote 'This car needs 134a by 1
January 1991.' We all had to walk past the
picture every day and it really brought home
to us what we had to achieve (see Figure
7.3).

Of course there were times when things
didn't go right. We frequently wanted things
from the rest of the business that they
weren't used to supplying and always in
double-quick time. That's where we learned
the importance of explaining what it was we
were trying to achieve, going out of our way
to make contact with people. Once we had
made that initial contact and showed we
appreciated people's efforts, we usually built
up a good relationship and could go back to
them again and again.

We also celebrated successes and milestones. We got a lot of interest from the media for our project. I appeared on *Blue Peter* (a popular BBC children's programme) to explain the work and got a Blue Peter badge. When I got back we put the badge up in the lab. It helped remind us we were working for future generations, not just for ourselves.

After four years of intense innovative activity, the first commercial size KLEA 134a plant in the world was commissioned in October 1990, three months ahead of schedule. The team had overcome all the inevitable negativity that accompanied its initial efforts.

A top creative team: the story of Flowcrete Plc

We have spoken a great deal about the importance of a constructive climate in stimulating creativity. Often this can sound like a 'never-never' land concept which is fine in theory but impossible in practice. In this case we describe the development of a company that places creativity at the heart of its management ethos.

Flowcrete Plc is one of the foremost manufacturers of specialist non-resin floorings in the UK. Founded by Peter Gibbins, an industrial chemist, in the 1980s, the company supplies specialist high-durability floor finishings to flooring contractors for the food, pharmaceutical and aerospace industries. Now based in Sandbach in Cheshire, they have offices in Hong Kong, Malaysia and the Czech Republic and are heavily involved in major construction projects throughout the world. Having recently acquired a supporting technology company, they are now floated on the stock market with a turnover recently surging past the £10 million mark.

This growth started from small beginnings. In 1982, Peter was joined in the business by his daughter Dawn, then 22, with little business experience but a great deal of enthusiasm for her father's work. Undaunted by her lack of technical knowledge, Dawn has taken the business forward and it is through her eyes that we see the Flowcrete story.

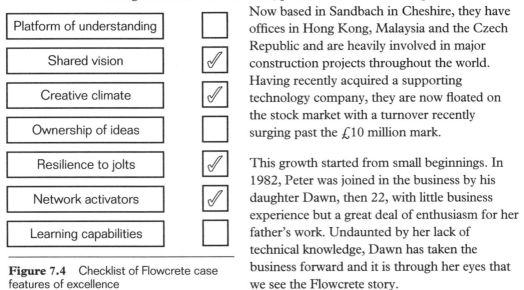

Figure 7.4   Checklist of Flowcrete case features of excellence

A VISION OF A BETTER STATE

Dawn was motivated to join her father partially by her irritation at his continual loss of intellectual property to other companies. She recalls:

> Bigger companies would come to Dad with problems regarding the durability and performance of their floor finishes. Dad would solve the problem, and then receive virtually nothing for his ideas. I suggested I come and work with him, to try to make some money!

They set up a small manufacturing site in a unit on an industrial estate and Dawn began to market the products. Eight years on, tragedy was to strike. Peter developed lung cancer and died two years later. If anything, his death spurred her on, as there was evidence that his illness resulted from exposure to the toxic substances present in the resins they used. Dawn became determined that the Flowcrete products, manufactured without dangerous solvents, would save others from a similar fate.

Like all entrepreneurs, she battled constantly to manage a growing business with erratic cash flow. From the beginning, she showed an intuitive understanding of the ways to stimulate creativity in those around her.

> I always try to be positive and cheerful in the factory and at home, even if things aren't going well. They say 'misery loves company' and it's true. If there is an atmosphere of gloom around the place it spreads very quickly and makes everybody low. We have achieved what we have by working hard to understand our customers and contractors. That means constant attention to detail and always asking ourselves 'Can we do better?' You can't do that if you don't have people willing to make the effort.

> I never pretend something is easy when it's not, and I don't kid people that I like something when I don't. I think everyone knows that I really want us to do well and I can't do things by myself. That means that sometimes I take a deep breath and let my staff try something, even if I'm not totally sure it will work. If it doesn't, then we sit

down and try to work out why. The day we
stop trying, we're dead.

Dawn realized very quickly that her qualities – enthusiasm for the products,
an ability to communicate with her suppliers and contractors, networking to
gain business contacts – were fine for raising the profile of the company, but
were not enough to keep everything going. For a while she had the unofficial
help of Mark Greaves, her husband, who had the experience of an MBA
undertaken at Manchester Business School. Mark gave what advice he
could, while working with another company. She combined running the
company with raising a family and after five very tough years things were
looking bright. Then there was a major setback.

DISASTER STRIKES

Dawn discovered that one of her contracts managers was failing to deliver
the quality of service required. She only discovered the problem when a
dissatisfied customer contacted her to complain. On investigation it became
clear that there was a significant problem with the contracts division and that
the manager had been diverting letters of complaint sent to the company.
For Dawn, this discovery was devastating. Contract cancellations meant that
the company had lost 50 per cent of its turnover in six months.

> We had a very serious situation to deal with.
> We had an unsecured £150,000 loan from
> the bank, and without the contracts we were
> unable to repay. The worst thing was that I
> had to make our contracts section, all very
> good people, redundant because we decided
> to pull out of that aspect of the business.
> They had worked really hard for us and it
> was heartbreaking. I was pregnant with my
> second child and it seemed as if everything
> was going wrong at once.

> We pulled together as a team and got
> through an extremely rocky period. The
> bank was very helpful and they could see
> that we were working hard to deal with the
> situation. We let all the staff know what was
> going on and I learned then that it really
> helps to be honest with people.

> I had to take responsibility; it had never

occurred to me that anyone who worked with us could be so dishonest. In my naiveté I had assumed that everyone was like me and this experience taught me to be more cautious in my dealings with people. It also taught me about the importance of focus in the business. Our expertise was in manufacturing the flooring, not in laying it on site. Contracting had stretched the business too far and we couldn't manage it properly.

By extending the marketing of the flooring processes, Dawn managed to increase turnover and gradually the company moved back into the black. Mark had agreed to come to work in the business as Marketing Director and they also recruited a Chief Executive, Phil Hogan, an MBA colleague of Mark's. Phil delivered a stern message to Dawn at their first board meeting.

It was the issue of focus again. Phil said that we had too many products aimed at too many different markets. We were still inclined to take a contractor's interesting problem and come up with an innovative solution, which was very time-consuming and didn't pay us enough. I am always very keen to try new things, and sometimes I get carried away! Phil suggested we needed to make some hard decisions about where we put our effort, otherwise we couldn't get the stability to grow. So we cut back on our lines, and put more effort into developing what would appeal to our main customer base.

'IS THAT A BONFIRE OVER THERE? NO, FLOWCRETE'S ON FIRE!'

Following its restructuring, the company consolidated its position and began to export to Malaysia and Singapore. Dawn continued to balance work and family life and took up horse riding for relaxation. It was on a journey back from the stables with her children that she pulled into a petrol station and saw the glow of a fire in the distance.

I asked the attendant if there was a bonfire on that night. She looked at me and said, 'No, Flowcrete's on fire.'

My heart stopped. I raced to the car and drove as quickly as I could to the factory. The fire engines were already there and the fire officer in charge told me to stay back as they were afraid the whole building would explode. After two hours the fire was put out and we could see that the factory was totally gutted.

The shock didn't really hit home for about 48 hours. We had so much to do. Our immediate priority was to get a Portakabin on site and set up telephone contacts. The fire happened on Saturday. By Monday morning at 8.30 we had our phone lines ready to answer customer queries.

The staff was fantastic. All our stock had been destroyed but our workers could remember most of the orders and the deadlines. We contacted all our main customers that first day and by the end of the week we had a skeleton production line up and running in temporary premises. During the next three months we found new premises and were thrilled because we didn't lose a single customer. All our work at keeping good customer contact really paid off.

The investigation revealed that the fire was caused by arsonists. We had lost many of our records and had to reconstruct our systems and in some cases build new ones. That proved to be an opportunity to introduce a new inventory control system and to upgrade our office management systems. Of course, it wasn't all plain sailing.

We had a fireproof safe, with our entire
wage records and accounts in it. We had to
smile when the fire officer asked for the key;
it had been in my secretary's desk! Many of
the records were smoke damaged and many
an hour was spent trying to decipher them. I
think the fact that we had worked so hard to
get back into action helped us with our
customers who could imagine the impact of
such a disaster. It was a difficult time but we
got through it and what we learned has
made the business stronger.

SPREADING THE CREATIVITY GOSPEL

From her story so far, it is clear that Dawn Gibbins is no ordinary
businessperson. She has achieved a high profile for her company, although
she started with a non-technical background, working in a business which is
almost totally male-dominated. Her belief in her product, and her
willingness to listen to suggestions from any quarter, illustrate a working
example of a creative climate. The company also seeks to emphasize the
importance of a 'whole life' attitude to business. The newsletter sent to all
customers and contacts carries features on stress management,
aromatherapy and diet for a healthy lifestyle. As a recent promotional
feature, Dawn sent out over a thousand wooden massagers in the form of
spiders in the Flowcrete colours.

Following the recent company acquisition, Dawn organized a Western
theme night, inviting all the staff of both companies to attend. In costumes
supplied by the company, all those who attended tried sharp shooting and
line dancing with the emphasis on team participation. It was a night enjoyed
by everybody, with a serious purpose behind it.

SEARCHING WIDELY, CHOOSING WIDELY

The Flowcrete story has been presented from Dawn's point of view. She is
the first to acknowledge that the growth and success of the company (and its
survival during the crisis times) stems from the teamwork shown by
everyone regardless of whether they are on the board or the factory floor.
The openness to ideas and willingness to experiment within a clearly defined
focus are clues to the company's continuing success.

Top Jobs on the Net

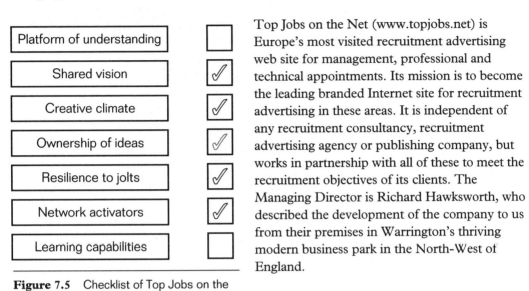

Platform of understanding	☐
Shared vision	✓
Creative climate	✓
Ownership of ideas	✓
Resilience to jolts	✓
Network activators	✓
Learning capabilities	☐

Figure 7.5 Checklist of Top Jobs on the Net case features of excellence

Top Jobs on the Net (www.topjobs.net) is Europe's most visited recruitment advertising web site for management, professional and technical appointments. Its mission is to become the leading branded Internet site for recruitment advertising in these areas. It is independent of any recruitment consultancy, recruitment advertising agency or publishing company, but works in partnership with all of these to meet the recruitment objectives of its clients. The Managing Director is Richard Hawksworth, who described the development of the company to us from their premises in Warrington's thriving modern business park in the North-West of England.

RICHARD'S STORY

Before Top Jobs on the Net, I was working for Hyperion Software, a half a billion-dollar software business worldwide. I enjoyed helping grow the UK subsidiary from very small beginnings, but it became too process-oriented for me. My boss there, Victor, left and bought into The Corporate Net which owns Top Jobs on the Net. A year ago in February 1997 I joined him, and we eventually brought over two other colleagues. We didn't have a brochure, we were struggling with cash flow all the time, but it was important right from the start that we could talk to the corporate world and be taken seriously. Although we were only a small company we needed to make our clients feel comfortable with our service. We have to sit across the table from them and be on equal terms.

COMMUNICATING A NEW KIND OF BUSINESS

When we first started we had several key propositions to put to the market. We offer a new way for companies to do their recruitment advertising and we had to help clients understand that the Internet was a viable proposition and as straightforward as using the traditional press. We had to de-emphasize the technological aspects of our proposition and communicate a solid business case. We also decided that if we were going to be a major long-term success around the world we would have to give high priority to branding and developing a global brand.

THE CREATIVE CLIMATE

I've been able to inspire people with what we can do. I like conflicts, they show that things are happening. I think they're essential for creative output. I look for energy and a can-do attitude in people. For example, in his first week with us our PR manager collared the Deputy Taoiseach at an exhibition in Dublin and got a photo opportunity on our stand. He got us on the Republic's main television channel too.

I've noticed that when we recruit new people for our teams, they joke and tease each other. Occasionally they have quite vocal rows about professional differences of opinion and then they make up when they've calmed down. Essentially I and my managers encourage quite a frothy environment where colleagues have a great deal of respect for each other but aren't obsessed by politeness. Too much politeness can keep a lid on the creativity. However, there's no backstabbing. I have had that in teams and it is death to the whole creative output of the team.

People don't want to go back to the old ways. They don't want to be shoehorned. The people who came to Top Jobs on the Net from Hyperion had creative discontent; the freedom to create is a key source of job satisfaction for them. At the time we couldn't offer the same package as Hyperion but they came because they had more space to create a new business. Money can't compensate for that. Take Kay, our Head of Marketing. She always takes a long break at Christmas to spend time with the extended family and her husband and four children. She told me that in previous jobs every year she never looked forward to coming back; she wanted to be a mother and do other things. This year for the first time after her holiday she was looking forward to coming back; her creative energy was relishing the challenge.

A NETWORK OF MAVERICKS

To be successful with creativity you often need to be a bit of a maverick, to bend the rules to push things through. In a former company, we had a customer conference every year somewhere in Europe. This was viewed as a flagship three-day event and the European board was very protective of it. However, feedback from our UK customers told us that a simple condensed one-day conference in London would be preferable.

My senior managers on the European board said don't do the one-day conference. They said that it would detract from the main conference, that customers wouldn't be willing to take time to attend both. I went ahead anyway and it was a success. Also, as the UK team had suspected, the customers liked the one-day event so much they booked for the main conference as well.

Sometimes you have to have confidence in your own knowledge of your business and take the risk of upsetting your superiors.

Recently I've seen the maverick approach in some of our blue-chip clients. We had quite a phenomenal challenge at Top Jobs on the Net. We wanted to ensure that our brand was the one that logged in people's minds as the brand for Internet recruitment. The obvious way was to supplement our marketing communications programme with prime-time advertising on a national network. There was one big snag; we didn't have any money! We thought of the idea of sharing the costs of the advertising with our customers. But how could we turn a fairly lame proposition into something that would excite enough customers to make the campaign a viable proposition? We needed something creative. After all, we were attempting something that had never been done before anywhere in the world.

We put together a business proposition that emphasized the value of a combined television and Internet recruitment advertising campaign. It was a world first. I visited 25 of our key clients – nearly all household names. The proposition was sound, and the first client we visited, Dell Computers based in Limerick, Ireland, agreed to join the campaign. After that, I had a series of 'nos'. Everyone thought it was a good proposition but in many cases couldn't see a way through the corporate jungle to get the approval. Eventually we did get five participants which was the number we had targeted in order to run the campaign.

It struck me that the people we had met at the participating organizations had something in common. Firstly they felt a degree of empowerment within their organizations to put their own companies on TV. These, remember, were Human Resources people not Marketing or PR. Secondly the people had personal characteristics which may have been a little maverick, they were all strong characters and not afraid to push through their ideas for the ultimate success of the organization. In one case, a major bank – not usually the kind of organization renowned for its creativity and innovation – I was dealing with a Director of Personnel. He seized on the idea and with his department pushed the TV advertising through. Later, as we were about to deliver the tapes to Channel Four, we found that the corporate PR people had only just learned about the campaign. They were a little peeved and we had a few anxious hours while we waited to see if they would pull the plug. They didn't, because it was a very advantageous deal for the bank and it had been pushed along so far.

Across the UK and Ireland there are people in large bureaucratic organizations who have this maverick instinct. I'm sure a lot of the progress that UK Plc makes is down to this network of mavericks.

KEEPING THE CREATIVITY GOING

I've got one nagging doubt about creativity in the British context. British management finds it hard to understand the importance of projects that can't be seen to be adding to the bottom line in the current year. The long-term success of an organization is built on the creativity of its teams and sometimes the cost of this doesn't sit easily with bottom-line performance. In my view, the best managers are those that have the courage to provide an

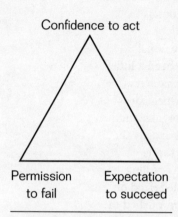

Confidence to act

Permission
to fail

Expectation
to succeed

Figure 7.6 Richard's model for team development

umbrella for their teams and create an environment that encourages creativity.

I think there are three virtues that help promote creativity. You can give people the chance to achieve by showing you've got confidence in them, by expecting them to succeed and by giving forgiveness if they fail. Room to move and freedom to make their own decisions, once you have the guidelines, is really important. It comes down to trust. You recruit people in the belief that they will do the job for you. You trust that they will work hard for you, and act with the interests of the company at heart. If you place genuine trust in people, they will perform.

VISION OF THE FUTURE

Something I've been able to do virtually all the time is to keep people going by saying 'We will be the most recognized recruitment brand in the world.' We've always had a clear idea where we are going. As long as everyone is clear on the vision their creativity will always move the business in the same direction. I remember when we moved into these new offices, which are light years ahead of where we started behind a soap factory in Salford, I said to Victor, the Chief Executive, 'I bet you didn't see us moving somewhere like this so soon.' He said, 'Yes, I did. I always did.' The stronger the vision, the stronger the urge to create and the stronger the success.

8 CREATIVE NETWORKS IN ACTION

A police force faces pressures to work more closely with its local community and with the many kinds of community services within it. A multinational giant encourages steps for stimulating creativity across its various sites. A task force within the US military recommends a 40-year plan to sustain its innovation. The directorate of a public works organization in the Netherlands aims to involve the public in thousands of consultation exercises within a few years of a successful pilot of the scheme. A group of IT managers meets regularly to explore ways of creatively influencing the implementation of their projects.

These examples are reported in this chapter. What they have in common is a core team with a shared vision or mission focused on the needs of a wider network. In contrast, the wider network included many so-called stakeholders whose members do not have a shared platform of understanding. Nor does it have the same level of cohesiveness found in a project team that performs regularly to a shared goal. Nor is it generally possible for the multiple experiences within the network to be easily assimilated into learning gains.

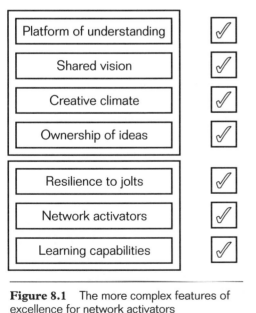

Figure 8.1 The more complex features of excellence for network activators

Our understanding of dream teams can still be relevant. Here, however, we have to address external factors. The core team still has the challenge of developing dream-team characteristics. Through its own training, and reflection on its experiences in the wider network, it may well achieve excellence in the seven factors, as shown in Figure 8.1.

In much of its work, the team is concerned with bringing together groups from the wider network, often in one-off events. Each of the temporary teams will have a unique platform of understanding, vision or goal, climate and potential owners of ideas. The temporary teams are therefore at the early stages of development. The process can be seen as one in which the network activators have the

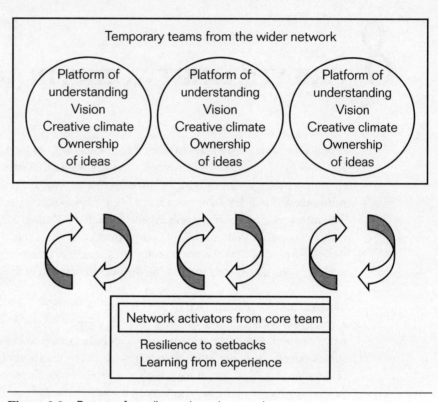

Figure 8.2 Pattern of excellence through network activation

creative leadership role of accelerating the transition through the form and storm stages within one-off team sessions.

Sometimes the first experiences are powerful learning jolts, which will leave the participants with a long-lasting shift in learning and understanding. However, as shown in Figure 8.2, we have to distinguish between the core team, which may have the seven characteristics of creative teams, and the temporary teams that will have differing platforms of understanding, visions, climates and idea owners.

The core team has a greater capacity to learn from its experiences within the wider network. Also, there will be more shared experiences within the core team together with the psychological and technical resources to deal with the inevitable unexpected jolts experienced in the networking activities. Putting these features together, we can understand the dynamics of network activators operating as shown in Figure 8.2, which will help us to appreciate what is going on in the case studies we are about to encounter.

May the force be with you . . .

There have been significant changes in the way police work is being carried out in the UK. Force organization has been decentralized to make it more responsive to local conditions and officer ranks have been reduced and posts amalgamated to produce a 'flatter' organization. These changes have led to the participation of officers and civilian personnel in problem-solving activities at a level never before seen in the service. To help implement these changes, we were asked to work with one police force to introduce some group creativity techniques.

The force in question comprises 5 200 police officers and 2 100 support staff, making it the fourth largest in the UK. Policing an area of 780 square miles containing densely populated urban and less well populated rural areas, it has faced all the challenges possible for a modern police force.

Our work was part of a major initiative to equip the police and civilian staff for the reorganizations ahead. Chief Superintendent David Lloyd, directing the Force Training School, realized that training and experience in group facilitation would be needed to enable the many types of consultative processes to take place. We concentrate here on the MPIA training although training in a wider range of skills was provided.

The first group of 14 participants was recruited by placing an advertisement in the force's official newsletter, the *Official Bulletin*. Chosen to give a cross-section of experience, the participants were from all areas of the force and included driving school instructors, firearms officers, operational detectives and IT specialists. Our initial programme sponsor was convinced that to take advantage of the opportunities arising from the changes, different group work approaches were needed. However, the design and delivery of the pilot creativity training was not influenced by the content of other training programmes.

The first two-day creative problem-solving programme was based on the MPIA model and the creativity techniques covered in Chapters 4 to 6 of this book. Three months after the programme, a progress workshop was held. The evaluation is best told in the words of the participants.

Don, a Chief Inspector in the Force Training School, had led several sessions dealing with force reorganization issues. He reported as follows:

> The main thing I found was that the
> MPIA gives confidence to my groups.
> They know that we won't be brainstorming
> for ideas all day. The spider diagram
> helps me to get the people in the group
> talking. Being able to put everything down
> and then look at it again later means we keep
> moving.

Jeff, a superintendent in charge of a large operational police station, found two aspects of particular value:

> We can all remember 'No clay pigeon
> shooting.' The group pick it up themselves
> and they tell each other when they think
> someone is being negative to ideas.
> 'Wouldn't it be wonderful if . . . ?' is great
> because it helps the team to be much more
> lively with their ideas. In my sessions I've
> had people of all different ranks and
> sometimes the junior officers feel slightly shy
> about putting in more unusual suggestions.
> The WIBWI, as we call it, helps to loosen
> things up.

An unusual aspect of the police situation is the mixture of police and civilian personnel. Traditionally, the police personnel have been to the fore in policy issues and one of the changes has been to introduce more civilian input. One of our civilian participants, Wendy, had been in the thick of sessions with high-ranking police personnel and civil agencies all in the same teams. She commented:

> I found the spider diagram and the How
> Tos really helpful. In the beginning the
> clashes of opinion shown in some of the
> How Tos was a bit frightening. I used the
> Yes And approach to help the different
> members find ways of working together.
> The really great thing was that after the first
> session the team members remembered the
> 'No clay pigeon shooting' and started to say
> it themselves!

> 1 Hold a pre-training briefing with your sponsor
>   to clarify roles and responsibilities for action
> 2 Ensure the right people are in the proposed creative
>   team
> 3 Start the meeting with clarification of goals and roles
> 4 Spend time on the spider and How Tos before idea
>   generation
> 5 Trust the structure to get you through unexpected
>   team difficulties

Figure 8.3   Guidelines for meeting facilitators.

Our police trainees had used elements of the creative problem-solving approach in their facilitation and group training to put together their own guide for force facilitators. Their main recommendations to others undertaking facilitation work are listed here and in Figure 8.3.

> Have a pre-session briefing meeting with your client, to make sure that they understand what your role as a facilitator is, and that *they* are responsible for taking the ideas forward.
>
> Explain very clearly to the group you work with that you are there to help them to make progress. Good work is the responsibility of everyone present.
>
> If you are dealing with a complicated issue, allow plenty of time for the spider diagram and How Tos so that the idea generation is clear.
>
> If all else fails stick to the structure, it will get you through!

EXTENDING THE CREATIVITY TRAINING

Over the next four years another 30 personnel took the two-day creativity course, together with selected aspects of the other training approaches. All the training given has been used to work with many different groups on a variety of issues. The growing emphasis on multi-disciplinary approaches to policing issues, particularly drug-related crime and serious burglary, has meant that the force facilitators have to deal with groups of social workers, probation officers, civic leaders, as well as force personnel.

From a standing start the role of the facilitators has grown, so that in 1997 they dealt with over 50 different assignments. To coordinate and ensure quality of work, the management support department has evolved a facilitation management service that would be the envy of many professional management consultancies.

COORDINATING THE REQUESTS FOR FACILITATED MEETINGS

Very early on, the importance of clarity about the role of the facilitator, the nature of the subject to be dealt with and the needs of the client requesting the work became apparent. Two members of the management support staff based at the force headquarters have taken the responsibility of managing the process. Eve takes the requests for facilitators and Sue manages the debriefing after the event. They describe their work in the following way.

> Eve: When people want a facilitator they call me and I ask them what type of meeting it is, how many people will be there and the venue. I try to match the facilitators to the event, taking into account experience and so on. For a standard event I usually work to a ratio of one facilitator to eight to ten participants. This will depend on the type of session being planned. Ideally I would like three weeks' notice of the event but this doesn't always happen. Over the past year we have received more and more requests for facilitators. Once people have attended a facilitated event and see the benefits, they are completely converted. We recently advertised for additional facilitators to be trained and received over 100 enquiries. Thirty-eight returned their completed forms and 16 have now gone through the training process.

WHAT A FACILITATOR NEEDS TO FALL BACK ON

In April 1997, the force was asked to facilitate a national visioning conference for chief police officers and representatives from government agencies on the future of IT in support of the police service. A team of four facilitators involved the group of 40 participants in a three- day idea generation process. The event was widely considered to have been a great success and had resulted in one of the most productive meetings that the participants had ever experienced together. One facilitator wryly summed up the experience as follows:

An event like this requires considerable planning, but no matter how much preparation you make you will always need to be able to think on your feet. Being able to fall back on good facilitation grounding is a vital safety net – and being able to fall back afterwards on a comfortable bed is also essential!

Sue: We have put together feedback sheets to get the reactions of the client who asked for the facilitation and the participants the facilitators have worked with. There is also a report-back sheet for the facilitator which is a debrief exercise allowing the facilitator some time to reflect on the session. Most of the feedback from the participants is positive. For many of them it is their first experience of being facilitated and they find that it helps them to get a lot done. Most report that they enjoy the communication with the group and listening to each other's views. The facilitators use their debrief forms to help other facilitators to learn and plan their sessions.

CONTRIBUTIONS TO ORGANIZATIONAL DEVELOPMENT

In 1995 a five-year programme was initiated for improving the force's core processes. The approach engaged front-line staff and stakeholders from across the whole system. They became involved in the redesign and implementation of changes to working practices, with the aim of improving performance. Each of the projects was sponsored by an assistant chief constable and was supported full time by the trained facilitators. The types of projects involved included:

- Call handling (how calls to the force by the public are prioritized and handled).
- Case handling (how criminal case files are correctly constructed for processing through to submission to the Crown Prosecution Service).

- Intelligence development (the compilation of all types of information from all sources within the force to provide a comprehensive intelligence capability).
- Crime investigation and management (how a crime investigation process should progress and be managed).

The programme review has provided plenty of scope for creative teamwork. In the case of the call handling project, using a number of approaches including the MPIA, 109 recommendations were made, ranging from minor improvements to radical changes. One such change was the introduction of a 'golden number' for non-emergency calls still requiring some form of police attendance. This has reduced demand on the 999 service.

The intelligence development project implementation team organized 27 walk-through presentations throughout the force area, reaching 700 further staff to engage in a debate about the impact of proposed changes. This resulted in a further 70 suggestions which were incorporated into the final process design. It is planned that two-thirds of the recommendations will be implemented within a year.

One very senior participant summed up the process as follows:

> The use of facilitated large groups in this process has led to robust design and a commitment to make things work, through involvement and recognition that we are all part of a wider system. Getting the right people involved together and helping them, through facilitated workshops, to come up with ways of working has brought about successful change. It has sent a powerful message throughout the organization about how we do business.

'Working with the grain': introducing team creativity within a mature organization

Procter and Gamble (P&G) is an interesting case to study for creative teams in action. The bulk of its income comes from very mature markets. Perhaps because of this focus, and the sheer scale and global reach of its operations, it has sometimes been accused of operating a very large and traditionally hierarchical structure. A study of P&G might help to answer the more general question of whether large global firms in mature markets can actively support creative team activities.

The company began in 1837 when William Procter, a candlemaker, and James Gamble, a soapmaker, combined forces in the newly booming town of Cincinnati, Ohio. A century and a half later the company still had its original name and headquarters location, but it had grown to global prominence with operating plants in nearly 50 countries, 80 000 employees and sales in about another hundred countries. Those sales had totalled $21 billion with earning in excess of £1 billion at the start of the 1990s. One often repeated corporate in-joke is that IBM stands for 'I've Been Moved', and that P&G stands for 'Pack and Go'.

One area in which P&G's creativity is highly visible lies in its branding; another is in its world-class manufacturing facilities. Yet the growth has been remarkably disciplined, with keen attention paid to the traditional skills of manufacture and branding of a relatively small number of consumer 'hygiene' products with global influence. This focus means that the company exercises a great deal of discipline on product development, which may superficially appear to be a resistance to new ideas and a lack of success in 'obvious' creative outputs as products.

This is the context in which we will look at a product champion for team creativity and her efforts at stimulating creativity internal to P&G.

DEVELOPING A TEAM FACILITATION COMPETENCE

If Procter and Gamble does not fit everyone's stereotype of a creative organization, our guide Mary Wallgren might also challenge stereotypic beliefs about creative individuals. Mary conveys the confident and rather serious air of a successful legal executive or perhaps an anchor woman in a TV news show. Her mild manner belies a great deal of self-confidence which has been tested through the pressures of international responsibilities. As well as becoming involved as an effective change agent in P&G, she has served on the US creativity-networking organization PRISM which helps to coordinate national and international creativity conferences.

She became interested through an involvement in one of several structured creativity initiatives around the company. A two-day creative thinking programme had been acquired which concentrated on basic principles and techniques. Those interested in developing their skills were encouraged to gain further training to reach a level of competence in facilitating creative teams. The third level of training equipped the keenest facilitators to become senior trainers on the basic two-day programme.

Listening to Mary gives many clues to her success. We can be sure it is success in P&G's terms in the continued support given to creativity from a company well able to identify and eliminate wasteful projects. She has achieved her goals through working with the grain of the company structures.

> Find a sponsor who is really interested in creativity and who wants to effect change. It's a tactical error to exclude important senior people from the creative team session. Sometimes their presence impacts poorly on dynamics, but if they stay away the rest of the group won't get to decisions that the owner will give support to. You also need to work at getting the hierarchy of a plant or division on board if there is a call for creativity there. The commitment from the hierarchy will be vital long term.

This is not a challenging and paradigm-busting kind of agenda. Or, if it is, the paradigmatic power structures are gently led into change rather than being jolted out of complacency. The process of gaining and sustaining credibility is one that also seems to have been considered carefully. Mary is aware of reinforcing mind-sets against change that is seen as wacky or trivial.

> Always take on challenges that won't risk credibility. If you work on things seen as too frivolous or unimportant that can be bad. But if you go for the big headache, that might be a way of reinforcing that nothing can be done.

She considers it particularly difficult to work 'close to home' and suggests that you may need to bring in credibility through outsiders with a proven track record of creative team facilitation.

> The creative problem-solving process looks linear but it's possible to use it very flexibly. You can start anywhere in the process that seems right for the client. Use bits, and loop back. Sometimes I can't get the system into a group up front, so I use it personally, and only share ideas I get with the group. Then you can always learn and experiment with new techniques and tools so you are flexible in their use.

Thanks to the prudent strategy of working with the grain, the network of creativity supporters has sustained itself within the company.

Scope for creativity in the military sphere

In 1984 US Chief of Staff General Charles Gabriel set up a task force to look 40 years ahead. Out of seven areas identified by the task force, one was to sustain innovation. One of the most celebrated consequences was the initiation of creative teams within the Electronic Security Command (ESC) at San Antonio, Texas, under the command of General Paul Martin. The general saw a means of making ESC the most innovative and forward-thinking command in the USAF. Team member Dale Clauson now runs a School for Innovators in Houston, Texas. He recalls the way the goal was approached, and how a small innovation group was set up to promote the message to all 13 000 personnel.

> As the whole process begins with ideas we really pushed people to capture ideas. We'd say that ink fades too quickly on mental notes! We used Blue Slips [a version of using Post-its for idea collection]. Sometimes if required, we'd form what we called LRITs, Long Range Innovation Teams. Anyway, we would always commend looking at ideas in three ways, the PIN approach. What's positive, what's interesting, what's negative?

> We saw we could only be safe if we had lots of ideas, likely to be small but collectively with high impact. In RAF Chicklands [in the UK] we got to over 800 ideas with approval rates of 60 per cent, and nearly two-thirds of these have been actioned. Most were minor but there was the occasional big win that led to savings of hundreds of thousands of dollars, or even several million dollars.

> Some of the creativity has been directed towards military applications that remain top secret. Elsewhere the gains are recorded.

Other outfits had similar sorts of creativity programmes. The Office of the Surgeon General's Military Health Care had an innovation network that searched for new and better ways to provide health care. You could also find examples in the [US] Air Force Communications Command, Space Command and Training Command.

Clauson is not blind to the difficulties of introducing change, particularly in the military environment.

We decided the greatest hindrance to innovative ideas was middle management. They wanted to control their subordinates and protect their seniors. Some people have a hatred, fear or intolerance of innovation or change. If senior, then such people have to be removed. If they are lower in the hierarchy they have to be bypassed or won over.

We learned that telling people they were empowered didn't mean they would act. The culture was one where no one wanted to take a step that could not be shown to be right. Everything took longer than we expected. But the results are there. Thanks to top-down commitment the resistances were weakened. And we stuck to non-financial rewards. We used written notes of thanks from the Vice-Commandant – they were very popular and got displayed in the workplace. In the end innovation turned out to be succeeding in making things happen, linked to all aspects of organization.

Rijkswaterstaat and the Infralab networking approach

Rijkswaterstaat is the Directorate General of Public Works in the Netherlands. It has encouraged a form of creative teamwork in support of major policy-shaping and implementation. For example, in the fifth

CREATIVITY IN THE MILITARY

The military has actually been associated with idea generation for many years. Alex Osborn's work produced many gains for the US Navy through brainstorming as early as the 1950s. More recently in Europe, Commander Nils Bech of the Defense Center for Leadership in Gurrehus, Denmark, has been developing a range of concepts to support creative teamwork within large hierarchical organizations such as are commonly found in the military. His system draws on a version of MPIA (the Parnes-Osborn problem-solving system) as a means of encouraging each level of a hierarchy to reinterpret strategic goals according to their own action requirements.

Through a practical application of laddering of goals, Bech has produced a refinement to the concept of hierarchical operation. More typically it is accepted that leadership requires the creation of some shared vision. Less obviously, the provision of a 'top-down' vision may lead to an unreflective acceptance of that vision. For Bech, a 'handed-down' goal is always a temporary structure and one that calls for involved and creative reworking. His system is a good example of establishing a platform of understanding, and reflecting on assumptions and goals so as to enhance team development and learning.

European Conference on Creativity and Innovation in Vaals, in 1996, the directorate arranged a special creativity session with 50 delegates and four innovation team members from the Rijkswaterstaat.

Guido Enthoven specializes in community creativity and, among other achievements, he has pioneered work on the highly successful Dutch national Ideas Line. This collects suggestions telephoned in by the public and has been backed by extensive media coverage. Guido recalls various innovations attributable to the directorate.

> In 1996 a series of storms produced serious flooding for the Netherlands, whose countryside is well known both for its low-lying nature and for the skilfulness in water management through its barrier constructions. The Rijkswaterstaat had to act quickly. The impulse under such pressures is to dump all notions of consultation. Procedures had to be shortened. By way of compensation, the people involved, such as environmentalists, were invited to the table and enabled to participate at a very early stage. The experiences from this situation were very

positive. Interactive policy development is
one of the most promising ways of achieving
governmental innovation.

The general approach takes place in a process called Infralab. Hank Kune of the Rijkswaterstaat explains that the term stands for an infrastructure laboratory in which the users of a service are involved as early as defining the start of the planning.

The creative team in the Infralab involves
government and citizens working together.
The process is short and clearly structured.
All who participate are challenged to do so
actively and creatively.

The impact of the initial Infralabs has encouraged the network activators within the Rijkswaterstaat to develop a challenging shared vision. Their aim is to extend public participation exercises to cover all of its 4000 infrastructure projects.

Postscript

We hope the network activators of this chapter will not mind being called everyday heroes and heroines, for that is one way of acknowledging their achievements. For us, they are examples of what can be achieved, not in exceptional circumstances, but within commonly experienced organizational cultures.

We have not sought out the secrets of the most famous creative teams. Rather we hope we have indicated the practical steps that can support change. Sometimes the changes appear modest. The important question is whether any change at all would have occurred without some such activity. Our view is that without the everyday acts of heroism described, change would have been far more limited in scope and transient in time. As well as achieving their own shared visions, such activators offer hope for any other team interested in influencing changes outside its own boundaries.

9 PROJECT TEAMS IN ACTION

One dark February morning Peter Casey looked quizzically at us across the breakfast table of the Business School cafeteria.

'It's peat,' he explained. 'I've got a peat problem. I wondered if you had someone who could help.'

As it happened we had no expert who could look at his problem. What we did have was a team of MBAs interested in any industrial project in need of bright ideas.

'This would be perfect for our creativity project,' Susan suggested.

'It's a lot of peat.'

'How much is a lot?'

'About two million tons,' Peter said. 'We will be clearing it for the next five years. We will be getting peat out at levels that are more than the entire market in the country at present.'

'In that case you definitely need a creativity team,' Susan said firmly.

Peter looked as if he was prepared to try anything.

Overview

A great deal of our understanding of teams has arisen from projects developed in response to requests such as the one just described. The focus of this chapter is how teams trained to behave creatively tackle real-life organizational tasks. The cases were developed from our records within the so-called Creativity Challenge. As such there are some differences in emphasis from the cases of Chapters 7 and 8 (see Figure 9.1).

We have selected examples such as Peter Casey's peat that illustrate the principles behind the practice. Although the teams have been given one

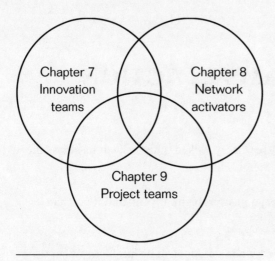

particular kind of training (with the MPIA approach) the lessons have direct relevance to those undertaking a task for a sponsor or client. The selection is intended to present practice, 'warts and all'. The teams would not make claims for being dream teams in their project work. They might consider that any exceptional results came from a combination of the opportunities provided by the project, the supportive environment in which they worked and the encouragement of the project sponsors.

Figure 9.1 Three overlapping kinds of teamwork

The creativity challenge

The Creativity Challenge operated in the 1990s as one among a series of options for our graduate students. Graduate teams from the Manchester Business School's MBA programmes had the option of taking part as a component of their business course. A typical team includes members drawn from international locations. All are graduates who intend to follow careers in business or business-related administrative occupations. Most members have had some years of experience in organizations, often as technical professionals such as engineers or accountants.

Each team works on a project that has been sponsored by one or more senior executives who expect a report of practical value. Time scales vary from a few days to two or three months. The project is assessed through written reports and a final presentation to the business sponsors and Business School tutors. The team is expected to demonstrate a grasp of practical details of the project and reasoned proposals for the sponsor to act on. It also has to indicate how the project process has been enriched by more conceptual knowledge connected with appropriate components of their MBA training.

Teams tend to comprise between four and eight members, sometimes established by self-selection. Often, though, the teams are assembled to ensure a wide range of backgrounds and a mix of genders and nationalities.

Sponsors tend to have responsibilities for the project under examination, and are able to indicate the current state of thinking in their organization and which proposals made by the team are plausible.

The overwhelming evidence is that the team and sponsors become quickly bonded and self-protective. In some ways there is little point trying to assess the distinct contribution of the MBA participants, because the effort is a combined one, strongly influenced by the involvement of the sponsors. In the final presentations, the sponsors sometimes leap to the defence of 'their' team against what they see as criticism from 'outsiders'. This makes our task difficult as quality assessors. We have to look behind the claims that the project will lead to significant future gains for the company. Our yardsticks are signals of the action-idea orientation and of team processes associated with a dream team in action.

In the early spring, therefore, our thoughts turn to firms who might have interesting projects for creative teamwork. We have received substantial help, including financial support from local sponsors and though our own network activators in large and small firms alike. The two selected examples typify the scale of contribution that can be made through such a creative team project.

Pete's peat

Casey's green and yellow vans are familiar features around Metropolitan Manchester. The Casey group is a multi-disciplinary construction organization. Its land reclamation company makes its money out of projects involving the removal of large quantities of materials from places where it is not needed to other places where it is less of a hazard. Like other land-fill specialists, Casey group has skills at excavation, quarrying and transportation in bulk quantities of solids and sometime liquids. Its work reshapes the urban landscape, effectively turning one set of holes in the ground into another set.

INTRODUCING PETER CASEY

The origins of the group can be traced to the entrepreneurial flair of its founder/owner Peter Casey. Peter had for some years acquired professional knowledge of publicly funded projects within a public works department. He had then built his own business on a regional basis and had watched and planned patiently as local and national politicians debated the North-Eastern continuation of the proposed Manchester Ring Road, the M66. He was as familiar as anyone with its geography and with the greatest challenges for companies in the business of landscaping and land-filling.

When the opportunity arose he was well prepared to make a competitive bid. P. Casey (Civil Engineering) Ltd tendered successfully for the land contract on a 250-acre site adjacent to the suburban town of Ashton-under-Lyne. The contract was large even for a well-established company of the size of the Casey group. It committed the group to develop the site by removing its topsoil and peat and then return the land to above its existing level to permit the building of offices and shops alongside a business park.

Preparing the contract helped bring into focus the rather special nature of the site. It offered both an opportunity and a potential problem for the Casey group. The opportunity was rather evident – to secure a long-term contract that would provide stable employment for a five-year period. The problem was that the site triggered strong emotions among conservationist groups. This was always going to require careful handling as Casey group had a genuine and long-term commitment to concern for the environment. The very title of the company's official history was Concern (ie, for the environment) which was summarized as 'pro-people, pro-progress, pro-environment'.

PETER ACQUIRES A CREATIVE TEAM

This was the background to Peter's breakfast visit to the Business School that February morning. In the previous year, a similar visit had resulted in him hiring Julie, a researcher in the Creativity Research unit, who had helped in the role of an independent observer of a logistics problem. Julie had been studying 'greening' and had been closely associated with the creativity work at the School. Now Peter wondered if he could be put in contact with another researcher to help with his pressing need for bright ideas to deal with his peat problem.

THE CREATIVITY TEAM IS ASSEMBLED

The deal worked out as follows. Peter would be provided with a problem-solving team whose members would have to produce ideas as part of their assessed project on creativity. This was allocated one day of their time a week over an eight-week period. Roughly half the time could be spent working directly on the peat project.

On his side, Peter agreed to give up some time to work with the team. This included on-site visits, problem-solving meetings and attendance at a final presentation. He also identified a director, Rupert Jorissen, New Development Manager, who would need to be involved. Rupert had considerable experience of the peat project, and was likely to be directly concerned with implementing any new ideas.

THE TEAM MEMBERS MEET

The first day of the assignment saw Peter and Rupert spend a few hours at the Business School explaining the project. The other team members had been briefed to resist the trap of moving too swiftly to 'solutions'. They were to remain at the M-stage of the MPIA model, accumulating information for mapping the scope of the project. After the meeting they would create a spider diagram of what they had learned.

In that first meeting, Peter and Rupert learned of the wide range of past experiences that the team members could bring to the project. They in turn communicated their willingness to work openly with the group. 'Both Peter Casey and Rupert Jorissen were extremely open, enthusiastic and helpful,' recalled one team member. 'Our "choice" of client proved to be very successful.'

At the next possible opportunity, Peter and Rupert took the team out for a 'briefing' which had been arranged in a nearby Chinese restaurant. It is safe to conclude that by the end of the meal, the team members had developed considerable mutual respect and willingness to work together. A great deal of bonding had occurred.

The team notes at the time revealed a particularly complex spider, verging on the multiple-leg mutant variety. After two visits to the site, the team decided to focus on searching widely for new ideas and markets for peat.

The brainstorming sessions inevitably proved to be highly productive. In fact, the team risked being swamped with ideas ('bogged down in peat ideas,' one member said), with no confidence that the closing-down process would be adequate. The members eventually found a matrix approach for analysing markets and attributes (Figure 9.2), a process that led to the selection of a few promising directions for further work.

Within the eight weeks allotted, a totally new export market of considerable promise had been found and the feasibility was being scoped. The original mind-sets were well on the way to being challenged. As well as considering 'How to find new markets' they began to consider 'How to get rid of two million tons of peat profitably'.

	Water	Absorbency	Energy store	Nutrients	Acidity
Commercial	☆	☆	☆	☆	
Horticulture	☆	☆		☆	☆
Water	☆	☆			
Soundproofing		☆	☆		
Sport	☆	☆			
Landfill		☆		☆	

Figure 9.2   Attribute/industry matrix for marketing peat

As is to be expected, the several hundred promising ideas were quickly sorted into those with particular immediate promise and the majority that could be shelved. The discipline of seeking action-ideas helped demonstrate which of the most exciting ideas were in effect 'blind alleys'.

THE IDEAS ATTRACT MEDIA COVERAGE

Projects are still under way within the company, so we must draw a veil over the most promising ideas. We are able to mention a few ideas reported in the final presentation, as these have already attracted considerable media interest, although they are likely to be more exotic than the ones that are now being applied to those two million tons of peat. It is a general feature of our creative idea presentations that the media tend to become excited about the most unexpected ideas despite the fact that these are often still at the 'Wouldn't it be wonderful if . . . ?' stage, destined to take many years' work and very often lead to ultimate abandonment. The exotic ideas (within the context of the then project) included soundproofing, water filtering and peat-based alternatives to mud baths. Landscaping for the 2002 Commonwealth Games in Manchester was also investigated.

One possibility which attracted particular media attention was peat for golf courses in Saudi Arabia. The vision for implementing that idea was summed up in the press photograph of Peter Casey apparently testing the peat surface of a golf tee, a team member teeing off, and a business professor in the background, weighed down with clubs, apparently acting as caddie.

THE MULTICULTURAL NATURE OF A PROJECT TEAM

An increasingly important aspect of life within international organizations is finding ways of managing multicultural teams. These may need particular support to work through the first stages (form and storm) of team development. The MPIA system offers a culturally neutral structure that lends itself well to these situations.

If managed constructively, the great variety of cultural and technical knowledge available can build a powerful platform of understanding for creative efforts. Dream teams may emerge. If left unmanaged, the process may founder. A common feature of teams from hell is the efforts by a dominant member to achieve results at the expense of wider team development of the seven factors associated with dream team performance.

The peat project had team members from Greece, the United States, Saudi Arabia, England and Norway. The benefits from 'searching widely' across their wide range of experience can be noted in the range of ideas developed.

Anniken had begun a working career in Norway. Her style with the group was rather quiet, which was unsurprising for someone who had to struggle more with the language than other group members. Her knowledge of shipping and of culturally different assumptions from her experiences in Scandinavian countries was to bring additional expert knowledge to the team although she considered herself toward the cautious side in suggesting and evaluating ideas ('I've got an administrative and analytical mind-set').

Bruce had a background in the construction and water industries. Perhaps as the English member of a team working for a British company he felt the responsibility of someone with specific expert knowledge. His final report suggested that he believed the group dynamics encouraged positive team spirit and yet reduced productivity.

Harry, from Greece, had already rightly acquired a reputation among his course colleagues as both a coordinator and someone very skilled in

information technology. He was to fill these roles admirably, and towards the end of the project bore the brunt of producing a sophisticated presentation using advanced IT facilities.

Jane had joined the team as an East-Coast American student with an interest in sales and marketing. Probably one of the most extrovert members of the team, she was able to encourage team building and ice-breaking with the sponsors with considerable skill and unobtrusive leadership qualities.

Michail, also from Greece, brought an interest in financial and transport industries to the group. His working style was somewhat reflective and he was inclined to think carefully before offering any idea – though this was then bound to have been well considered.

Uday was brought up in the Middle East and had extensive contacts in Saudi Arabia and The United Arab Emirates. This was to prove invaluable in working up an idea for exporting peat to luxury golf courses in the Middle East.

THE IMPORTANCE OF A CREATIVE SPONSOR

It is tempting for the creative team to be self-congratulatory about the success of 'their' efforts. We have found that successful teams sometimes overlook the importance of a sponsor who is willing to 'own the problem'. We might have overlooked the importance of this factor in the success of 'Pete's Peat' team if we had not come across this account of the team's sponsor, written some years earlier. It is taken from an introduction written in 1993 by Chief Superintendent Trevor Barton, Greater Manchester Police, for a corporate history entitled *Concern: an account of the first 25 years in the life of the Casey Group of Companies*.

> Peter Casey is a quiet man, thoughtful and always capable of carefully weighing up a situation before making a decision. It is this that has enabled him to build a company over the last 25 years from what was a one-man band to one of the most efficient and influential building, landscaping and civil engineering groups in the North of England.
>
> It is my opinion that many people easily underestimate the Casey attitude to business and life in general. If anyone has been through what is sometimes called 'the university of life' it is Peter, and he has developed a great ability to see and understand projects and schemes in the widest possible sense. He appreciates the value of his workforce and has the ability to weld them together as a creative team. We find that we are very much in agreement on well-known but often neglected principles, one to provide the best service, two to pursue excellence in every field, and three, always to respect the individual.

This kind of track record hints at the positive impact that the sponsor's attitude to change might have had on the overall success of the project. A similar conclusion on the sponsor's contribution might be reached in our next case example.

Lancashire Dairies

Jeremy Kearns, the Joint Managing Director, is the great-grandson of the founder of Lancashire Dairies. With his cousin Tim, he manages the company, which has been in his family since the last century. On the walls of his office hang the photographs of the previous managing directors. The family nature of the dairy is reflected in the fact that the directors know all their staff by name.

It was Jeremy who became interested in applying a creative thinking approach to his company. He had attended open days at the Business School, where he had seen the outcome of the method applied to a variety of business problems. He takes up the story.

> We are a well-established company with a good reputation in our business. We've always been interested in new ideas, and we always look to make the best of any assets we have. We are very proud of our flavoured milk products, which have given us the opportunity to export worldwide. Over the past couple of years the flavoured milk side of the business has really grown. During the summer we work flat out to keep up with demand. In the winter sometimes the lines are slack and we've often thought we'd like to find a way to keep the process going. We've talked about this in the dairy and I thought it would be a great idea if the MBA group could look at this for us.

THE COMPANY CULTURE

In the 1890s, J.J Kearns started up a small family concern in St Helens selling ten gallons of milk a day. He bought the milk directly from local farmers and distributed it throughout the region building a reputation as an honest tradesman, selling good milk at full measure (these were the days of adulterated food and variable weights and measures). By the 1920s the business had grown substantially and moved to a site in Mulberry Street, Manchester, close to the present-day premises. Throughout its history, Lancashire Dairies has maintained direct contact with its farmers and is still one of the few dairy distributors buying milk directly from dedicated farm suppliers. The family business thrived, surviving two world wars and innumerable changes in the dietary habits of its customers. About to enter the 21st century, the firm he founded is the largest independent dairy in the UK.

The company has always been sensitive to the needs of its customers. In the 1970s, it was the first to put fresh milk into plastic bottles and to introduce the screw-on cap, making it easier to drink milk 'on the move'. It is one of the few companies to have its own plastic bottle production.

Maintaining its reputation for innovation, the company was also one of the first to recognize the potential of the flavoured milk market. Its long-life flavoured milk drink, Superlife, is the market leader, and it is the only producer of long-life milkshake, marketed under the brand name Shake, Rattle and Roll. Present in garage forecourts, supermarkets and UK motorway service areas, the distribution has been boosted by the introduction of chilled vending machines – another first in the industry.

In the 1930s, the company had the opportunity to move to a central Manchester location when they bought the old ice skating rink, the Ice Palace. In the reception area, photographs of former ice skating champions share space with those of milk carts and dray horses in the crowded streets of Manchester, notable for the absence of cars. Away from the roar of traffic you enter a world of purposeful, measured activity. The milk is delivered daily and moved through the treatment and bottling plants. From behind thick transparent plastic curtains you see white-coated individuals checking temperature valves, monitoring the movement of the milk from one process to another. Throughout the dairy there is the hum of machinery and the hissing of steam.

THE PROJECT TEAM IS FORMED (JEREMY KEARNS' ACCOUNT)

We had our first meeting at the Business School and I explained the situation as best I could. Tony Price, non-executive director, came with me. It was the first time we had used something like the MPIA system and we were really curious to see how things would work out. The team told us that they would do an information map or spider diagram for us and that we could use it to discuss the options open to us. They visited the dairy and talked to some of the staff and

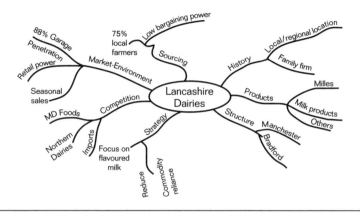

Figure 9.3   The Lancashire Dairies spider

the next time we met they had produced a spider diagram to show us the picture as they saw it.

When we had told our staff that the team would be working with us I think they were a bit sceptical about what they could achieve. When the team members came to the dairy and talked us through the spider diagram some of the doubts disappeared. It showed us just how complicated the situation was and how we had to think very carefully about any ideas we had because any increase in winter production could bring strain in the system somewhere else.

We were very excited by the progress the team members had made in understanding the situation, although all the information they had given us was a bit daunting! They had also done some data-based market research which helped us to have faith in what they were telling us. From the spider diagram they had gone on to find some How To statements which helped summarize the situation for us. We had a go with them at producing How Tos at the dairy. They reminded us, in the nicest possible way, that we shouldn't judge their suggestions too soon. When they had gone, we started to say 'No clay pigeon shooting' when we discussed the ideas on our own.

We started with 'How to utilize the surplus capacity company in the winter months', which was a fair summary of the position as we saw it. From there the team used lateral thinking to suggest 'Wouldn't it be wonderful if we could think of a product that would be non-seasonal in nature?'. This turned the situation on its head and removed the seasonality problem. This was good because we were locked into thinking about how to get round the seasonality issue, not removing it altogether.

After talking to us, the team worked in two main areas, developing new products and marketing our existing products in a more novel way. We discussed the criteria that any new ideas must meet for us to use them. We needed ideas that would use our expertise in flavoured milk and existing production resources. We didn't want to compete with any of our established products either.

After our criteria setting we were a bit worried that we had constrained the team too much. We needn't have worried. The team members came back with some extremely interesting ideas. They pointed out that we could look at distributing the milk in outlets not affected by the weather. For instance, in an aircraft, it makes no difference if it's hot or cold. The same applies for cinemas, trains and theatres. They also suggested that we consider sports sponsorship. Ice hockey is becoming big in Manchester and we obviously have links with ice sports through our premises. It's a high-energy sport, requiring high-energy drinks, and it's played in the winter, one of our quieter times.

They also suggested food drinks during the winter and special Christmas flavours. One we particularly liked was a Mocktail, a non-alcoholic cocktail, well designed and packaged, to be distributed to bars and pubs. We were really pleased with this, because the team had been enthusiastic about an idea we had to reject. This was to make alcoholic cocktails. The team had stressed the Yes And approach to ideas. We tried very hard, but all the Yes Anding in the world couldn't get us to take the idea on board. We felt that this was a product we just didn't want to make. The team took our rejection in good part, although we could see the members were really disappointed.

After our work with the team we started to pilot some new products. We really enjoyed working with them and we still remember what they told us early in the project: 'If you always do what you've always done, you'll always get what you've always got!'

We learned a lot about our business, and it was really interesting to get the team's impressions. I've worked in the dairy all my life and it's so much a part of me that it can be difficult to step back and see things objectively. I didn't always agree with the team and sometimes they had us talking about their ideas for days. When we finished the project, we really missed them.

Postscript: 'Wouldn't it be wonderful if . . . ?'

One of the features of creative teams is the development of a vision. Continuing our use of 'Wouldn't it be wonderful if . . . ?' vocabulary, here is one such dream.

Wouldn't it be wonderful if dream teams became the norm? Wouldn't it be wonderful if the secrets of dream teams stopped being a secret? Slowly at first, and then with increasing momentum, new structures and ideas are applied in organizations. A time comes when a majority of companies have discovered the benefits of applying the basic principles in teams and networks. Then even the companies most resistant to new ideas will accept the new norms of team behaviours.

Yes it would be wonderful – but is it ever likely to happen? Perhaps we should be permitted one last Yes And. Yes and it is not just likely. In one sense, the dream we describe has already happened in the case of the 'quality' movement. The basic idea of total quality was that work teams were an under-utilized resource. It proposed that such teams could be trained so that productivity could be greatly enhanced. It took a long time for the idea to be accepted, but now it is a worldwide phenomenon.

What happened to quality could happen to efforts to stimulate creativity in teams. Structured creativity approaches are growing in impact in many countries and in many kinds of work teams. All it needs is the continued development of a network of committed people and a willingness to put ideas into action at every possible opportunity. We hope this book will become a manual in that social revolution.

BIBLIOGRAPHY

In recommending these books we have tried to select those that are both valuable and easy for organizational professionals and trainers to obtain. In this respect, some less recent books that have been reissued are particularly noteworthy. They represent the most direct way to explore more deeply the ideas found in this book.

Adair, J. (1979) *Action Centred Leadership*, Epping: Gower Press. An influential practical approach to leadership from a distinguished military historian and business consultant.

Amabile, T.M. (1996) *Creativity in Context*, Boulder, Colorado: Westview. A most influential account of the nature of intrinsic motivation within the creative process.

Belbin, R.M. (1996) *The Coming Shape of Organization*, London: Butterworth Heinemann. An updated account of Belbin's well-known team-role theory.

Bennis, W. and Biederman, P.W. (1997) *Organizing Genius: The Secrets of Creative Collaboration*, New York: Addison Wesley Longman Inc. and London: Nicholas Brealey. Captures the elements of creative teamwork in case example format.

Carson, J.W. and Rickards, T. (1979) *Industrial New Product Development*, Farnborough, Hants: Gower. The early work leading to techniques for dealing with the thought-action gap. We have developed our current action-idea approach to team creativity from these early suggestions such as 'product-in-a-bottle' thinking.

Checkland, P.B. and Scholes, S. (1990) *Soft Systems Methodology in Action*, Chichester: J. Wiley. Peter Checkland's soft-systems approach encourages 'right-brain' development of insights into organizational situations.

Collins, J.C. and Porras, J.I. (1994) *Built to Last: Successful Habits of Visionary Companies*, New York: Random House.

Couger, J.D. (1995) *Creative Problem Solving and Opportunity Finding*, Danvers, Mass.: Boyd and Fraser. Dan Couger's last major work on creative problem-solving. It includes many techniques and practical examples in industrial and professional environments.

Csikzentmihalyi, M. (1988) 'Society, Culture, and Person: A Systems View of Creativity', in R.J. Sternberg, *The Nature of Creativity*, Cambridge: Cambridge University Press. Professor Csikzentmihalyi has conducted important studies into the nature of creative flow and the systemic nature of creativity.

De Bono, E. (1987) *Six Thinking Hats*, London: Penguin. A remarkably simple yet effective way of structuring team behaviours to creative effect.

De Bono, E. (1990) *I am right – You are wrong*, London: Viking. A lucid explanation of why cooperative skills are needed for organizational and social development, and how such skills can be fostered.

Ekvall, G. (1991) The Organizational Culture of Idea Management: A Creative Climate for the Management of Ideas', in J. Henry and D. Walker (eds), *Managing Innovation*, London: Sage Publications, pp73–79. The creative climate measure found to be associated with innovative performance in teams.

Geschka, H., Moger, S.T. and Rickards T. (eds) (1995) *Creativity and Innovation: The Power of Synergy*, Darmstadt, Germany: Geschka Associates.

Handy, C. (1988) *The Age of Unreason*, London: Hutchinson. Thoughtful, well-argued case for radical thinking in the service of social and organizational change.

Johnson, B. (1992) *Polarity Management: Identifying and Managing Unsolvable Problems*, Amherst, Mass.: HRD Press. A clear and practical account of managing tensions in teams.

Kirton, M.J. (1994) *Adaptors and Innovators: Styles of Creativity and Innovation*, (2nd edn), London: Routledge. Gives full details of the adaption-innovation work found valuable in team-building.

Koestler, A. (1964) *The Act of Creation*, London: Hutchinson. An excellent 'platform of understanding' on breakthrough or insight thinking.

Kolb, D.A., Rubin, I.M. and Osland, J.S. (1991) *The Organizational Behavior Reader*, (5th edn), Englewood Cliffs, New Jersey: Prentice-Hall International. David Kolb's early work on experiential learning helped us in our own ideas on how creative teams develop over time.

Larson, C.E. and LaFasto, C.E. (1989) *Teamwork: What must go right/What can go wrong*, Newbury Park, California: Sage. A careful study of a wide

range of teams mostly in US organizations arrives at similar sets of
success factors to those reported in our work here.

Morgan, G. (1993) *Imaginization: The Art of Creative Management*,
Newbury Park, California: Sage. Extends the author's more theoretical
work *Images of Organization*.

Parker, M. (1990) *Creating Shared Vision*, Ohio: Dialog International. A fine
case summary of a transformation process within an organization
brought about by creative leadership. The power of developing a shared
vision is spectacularly illustrated.

Parnes, S.J. (ed) (1992) *Source Book for Creative Problem-solving*, Buffalo,
New York State: The Creative Education Press. A comprehensive
survey of 50 years of work in applied creativity by a pioneer in the field.

Rickards, T. (1997) *Creativity and Problem-Solving at Work*, Aldershot,
Hants: Gower. The companion volume to this, concentrating more on
general business application of creative techniques.

Senge, P. (1990) *The Fifth Discipline*, New York: Doubleday. Influential and
coherent account of systems thinking as 'the fifth discipline'. Also serves
as a handbook of personal development skills for creative leaders.

Van Gundy, A. (1992) *Idea Power: Techniques and Resources to Unleash the
Creativity in your Organization*, New York: Amacom. Authoritative
compendium of creativity techniques including computer software
support systems.

INDEX

The Complete Guide to People Skills

Sue Bishop

As a manager wanting to get the most out of your team, you need to practise 'people-focused leadership'. You need to encourage your people to contribute fully to the success of your organization, and to do that, you need an armoury of people skills.

Sue Bishop's book provides a comprehensive guide to all of the interpersonal skills that you need to get the best from your team. Skills that you can apply in formal settings, such as recruitment interviews, or appraisals, as well as less formal, such as coaching or counselling. Team skills to help you communicate with, and develop, your people. Skills to handle disciplinary matters, or emotional crises, or to resolve conflict. And skills that you can use when you are just chatting with and enthusing individuals and the team.

The Complete Guide to People Skills is divided into two parts. Part I gives an overview of the core skills, and offers a brief explanation of some self-development and communication theories.

Part II shows how to apply these skills in different situations. It is arranged alphabetically by topic - from appraisals to teamwork. Each section includes an exercise to help you learn more about the skills and techniques and to apply them in your work.

Gower

The Excellent Trainer

Putting NLP to Work

Di Kamp

Most trainers are familiar with the principles of Neuro-Linguistic Programming. What Di Kamp does in her book is to show how NLP techniques can be directly applied to the business of training.

Kamp looks first at the fast-changing organizational world in which trainers now operate, then at the role of the trainer and the skills and qualities required. She goes on to deal with the actual training process and provides systematic guidance on using NLP in preparation, delivery and follow-up. Finally she explores the need for continuous improvement, offering not only ideas and explanation but also instruments and activities designed to enhance both personal and professional development.

If you are involved in training, you'll find this book a powerful tool both for developing yourself and for enriching the learning opportunities you create for others.

Gower

Proven Management Models

Sue Harding and Trevor Long

This unique volume brings together, in a standardized format, 45 models
for management diagnosis and problem-solving: all chosen for their proven
value to senior management and MBA tutors alike. They cover strategy,
organization, human resources and marketing, and range from well-known
techniques such as Breakeven Analysis and Situational Leadership to less
familiar approaches like Five Forces and the Geobusiness Model.

Each entry contains:

- a diagrammatic representation of the model
- the principle on which the model is based
- the underlying assumptions
- the issues involved
- guidance on using the model
- related models
- further reading.

The models are indexed by subject and there is also a matrix showing how
they are related to each other.

The result is a reference guide that will be invaluable to practising
managers, consultants and management students alike.

Gower

Gower Handbook of Management Skills

Third Edition

Edited by Dorothy M Stewart

'This is the book I wish I'd had in my desk drawer when I was first a manager. When you need the information, you'll find a chapter to help; no fancy models or useless theories. This is a practical book for real managers, aimed at helping you manage more effectively in the real world of business today. You'll find enough background information, but no overwhelming detail. This is material you can trust. It is tried and tested.'

So writes Dorothy Stewart, describing in the Preface the unifying theme behind the Third Edition of this bestselling *Handbook*. This puts at your disposal the expertise of 25 specialists, each a recognized authority in their particular field. Together, this adds up to an impressive 'one stop library' for the manager determined to make a mark.

Chapters are organized within three parts: Managing Yourself, Managing Other People, and Managing the Business. Part I deals with personal skills and includes chapters on self-development and information technology. Part II covers people skills such as listening, influencing and communication. Part III looks at finance, project management, decision-making, negotiating and creativity. A total of 12 chapters are completely new, and the rest have been rigorously updated to fully reflect the rapidly changing world in which we work.

Each chapter focuses on detailed practical guidance, and ends with a checklist of key points and suggestions for further reading.

Gower

Gower Handbook of Training and Development

Second Edition

Edited by John Prior, MBE

This *Gower Handbook*, published in association with the Institute of Training and Development, first appeared in 1991 and quickly established itself as a standard work. For this new edition the text has been completely revised to reflect recent developments and new chapters have been added on cultural diversity, learning styles and choosing resources. The *Handbook* now contains contributions from no fewer than forty-nine experienced professionals, each one an expert in his or her chosen subject.

For anyone involved in training and development, whether in business or the public sector, the *Handbook* represents an unrivalled resource.

Gower

A Systematic Approach to

Getting Results

Surya Lovejoy

Every manager has to produce results. But almost nobody is trained in the business of doing so. This book is a practical handbook for making things happen. And whether the thing in question is a conference, an office relocation or a sales target, the principles are the same: you need a systematic approach for working out:

- exactly what has to happen
- when everything has to happen
- how you will ensure that it happens
- what could go wrong
- what will happen when something does go wrong
- how you will remain sane during the process.

This book won't turn you into an expert on critical path analysis or prepare you for the job of running the World Bank. What it will do is to give you the tools you need to produce results smoothly, effectively, reliably and without losing your mind on the way.

Gower

Opportunity Spotting

How to Turn Good Ideas into Business Success

Nigel MacLennan

You know those inspired ideas your colleagues have that seem so obvious, you wonder why you didn't get there first? The secret to finding them is now open to you.

This book tells you how to cultivate a creative state of mind and how to recognize the value of your ideas when you come up with them.

Whether it's the search for new products and services or the need to adapt to rapidly changing markets, the company - big or small - that fails to exploit available opportunities is doomed. This unusual book sets out a systematic approach to opportunity-seeking. It provides strategies for generating ideas and exploiting openings in a wide range of contexts.

In addition to describing techniques for identifying opportunities, Nigel MacLennan shows how to recognize those with the greatest potential, how to overcome the inevitable barriers, how to turn promising ideas into actual revenue - and how to achieve an organizational culture in which everyone becomes opportunity-minded.

Gower

The Vision

Richard Israel and Julianne Crane

In the new global economy, where wealth is information and the rules of business have been turned inside out, a new force is emerging. It weighs three pounds, works 24 hours a day and has unlimited potential. Sounds like you should find out more? Well, you're already the proud owner of one. In fact, you are using it now.

Recent research has begun to reveal the mysteries of the human brain and its almost infinite capacity. *The Vision* provides a step-by-step guide to using more of your creative genius. It tells the fast-moving story of Sandy Stone, as she struggles to boost the performance of her sales team, battles with her unhelpful boss, teaches – and learns from – her young son. As you share Sandy's experiences you will learn with her:

• how to create and achieve a peak sales vision for more sales
• how to harness the power of your brain
• how to use multi-sensory thinking
• how to mind-map for improved memory and recall
• how to become a visionary leader
• how to change limiting belief systems (your own and other people's)
• how to enhance self-esteem, and how to manage your time
more effectively
• how to master the visionary process for future growth.

Gower